SHARING THE GOSPEL WITH MUSLIMS

A HANDBOOK FOR BIBLE-BASED MUSLIM EVANGELISM

by

JOHN GILCHRIST

First published 2003
New Edition 2009

Life Challenge Assistance Network
P.O. Box 50770
Nairobi 00200
KENYA
info@lifechallenge.de

OASIS INTERNATIONAL LTD

INSIGHT BOOKS
AFRICAN ISSUES AFRICA'S AUTHORS

Sharing the Gospel with Muslims

First Published 2003

ISBN: 978-1-59452-563-6
ISBN: 1-59452-563-3

Oasis International is a ministry devoted to fostering a robust and sustainable pan-African publishing industry. For more information, go to oasisint.net.

Sharing the Gospel with Muslims

Introduction

Using the Word of God in Muslim Evangelism

Muslim evangelism is one of the toughest fields of Christian witness. During the last two centuries Christians have sought to win Muslims to Christ, only to find that it is extremely difficult to persuade the sons of Islam that Jesus Christ should be their Lord and Saviour. In recent times mission agencies and Christian evangelists have proposed numerous methods guaranteed to make Muslim evangelism work, namely, to bring about the desired results. Friendship evangelism, relational evangelism, contextualisation, felt-needs approaches - they're all part of a catalogue of methodologies presented as the best way of effectively reaching Muslims for Christ. Planting churches among Muslims has become a subject of study, discussion and practical expression in many areas before any form of evangelism has even started. Results are the desired goal and, if possible, in sufficient numbers to establish Muslim convert churches.

Different methods of evangelism are one thing, promoting these in turn as the *only* ways Muslims can be reached is another. On the back cover of her book *Waging Peace on Islam* Christine Mallouhi says "When Muslims are sceptical of our creed, confused by our message and wounded by our warfare, the most credible witness left is our lives. Muslims need to see Jesus, and the only way most of them will see him is in us." Bill and Jane, missionaries in an Islamic environment who are not further identified, state in Phil Parshall's book *The Last Great Frontier*: "If the status quo is to change, a new way must be found whereby Muslims can come to Christ in the context of their own culture and community" (p.178).

The intense resistance of most Muslims to the Gospel has driven many Christians to find alternative ways of reaching them for Christ, ways that appear more likely to produce the desired results. In consequence a variety of different methods have been proposed, invariably coupled with dogmatic assertions, such as "this is the only way" or, alternatively, "we need a new way!" While the simple preaching of the Gospel has won over many millions of Hindus and other peoples to Christ, it seems to hit a brick wall with Muslims, hence the search for other methods apparently more guaranteed to bring about the desired end-result.

I recently listened to a Sunday morning sermon in my home church where the preacher stated very simply "You cannot build the kingdom of God. Only God can. You can only reflect it through your witness and life." That, to me, puts it in a nutshell. As the Psalmist put it so straightforwardly:

> Unless the Lord builds the house, those who build it labour in vain.
> *Psalm 127:1*

The field of Muslim evangelism tries and tests Christians very severely at this point. Are they going to trust God to do his own renewing work in calling out the sons of Ishmael to faith in Jesus Christ, or are they going to force the issue by finding human ways of persuading Muslims to become believers, often through methodologies which seem to dilute the costs of true discipleship? The Apostle Paul was very conscious of the fact that only God, through his Spirit, can draw anyone to himself and so he said to the believers in Corinth:

> I planted, Apollos watered, but God gave the growth.
> *1 Corinthians 3:6*

Jesus Christ himself delivered a parable which makes the very same point. While surrounded by his twelve disciples and many others who listened favourably to his teachings, he said:

> The kingdom of God is as if a man should scatter seed upon the ground, and should sleep and rise night and day, and the seed should sprout and grow, he knows not how. The earth produces of itself, first the blade, then the ear, then the full grain in the ear. But when the grain is ripe, at once he puts in the sickle, because the harvest has come.
> *Mark 4:26-29.*

God *alone* can give the growth. God alone can build the house. The man who plants, waters and reaps *knows not how* the seed sprouts and grows. God alone knows. Muslim evangelism needs a return to the simple witness of the Gospel, a one-on-one sharing of the great truths of the good news of salvation in Jesus Christ, and this book seeks to provide Christian evangelists with precisely that. It is a handbook of Biblical means of sharing the Gospel with Muslims, hence its title. It shows you how to use the Word of God to effectively communicate the great truths of our faith to willing Muslim hearers. It guarantees no results, it shows only how to witness to the grace of God in Jesus Christ from the pages of Scripture. It covers the whole Bible, from the creation of Adam to the second coming of Jesus. It leaves the results to God.

Over almost twenty years, in the nineteen-seventies and eighties, I was privileged to be part of a special group of young Christians seeking to share the Gospel with Muslims in our province in South Africa, the Transvaal. The province no longer exists for the provincial maps of South Africa have dramatically changed in the past ten years, but the Transvaal was the northernmost province sandwiched between Botswana, Zimbabwe and Mozambique. About 50,000 Muslims lived within its borders and we visited them from home to home in every city and town, covering virtually every Muslim home in the province excepting Lenasia near Johannesburg, where the largest Muslim community lives, which we only partially evangelised.

There were results, but they are not the theme of this book. Using the Word of God effectively in reaching Muslims for Christ is the theme, and the contents of this book record various ways we learnt over the years of witnessing to Muslims from the pages of the Bible, God's holy Word, and the supreme source which the Spirit uses to direct all mankind to the Gospel. Its value for this purpose is summed up in this verse:

> For the word of God is living and active, sharper than any two-edged sword, piercing to the division of soul and spirit, of joints and marrow, and discerning the thoughts and intentions of the heart.
>
> *Hebrews 4:12*

We also learned, however, from the pages of Scripture itself, that the most constructive way of using the Bible in witnessing to Muslims is to base our witness on the points of belief that we share in common with them, and to build a Gospel message on these subjects of common ground. We will look at this in more detail.

Paul's Examples from the Book of Acts

When Paul went into the Jewish synagogues scattered throughout Greece and Asia Minor, he was able to freely argue with all present, explaining and proving from the Scriptures that Jesus was the long-awaited Messiah. When he arrived at Athens, however, and looked around the city, he found himself in a very different environment. The city was full of idols and its markets were frequented regularly by Epicurean, Stoic and other philosophers. He was no longer on his own turf. How did he evangelise people from a totally different nation, culture and religious heritage? When he stood on the great Areopagus and was challenged to present his message to the locals who regarded what he had already preached as a strange new teaching, he began:

> Men of Athens, I perceive that in every way you are very religious. For as I passed along, and observed the objects of your worship, I found also an altar with this inscription, "To an unknown god." What therefore you worship as unknown, this I proclaim to you.
>
> *Acts 17:22-23.*

There are two important lessons to be learnt from this brief passage. Firstly, Paul *made himself acquainted with the beliefs of the people he sought to evangelise*. The best way of getting the impact of this principle is to accentuate certain words in his first sentence: "**I perceive** that in every way you are very religious. For as **I passed along** and **observed** the objects of your worship, **I found** also an altar with this inscription." Paul took time to familiarise himself with the background of the people he wished to reach. He *perceived*, as he *passed by* he also *observed*, and as he did so he *found* an altar.

In Muslim evangelism the Christian must learn as much as he can about the beliefs and practices of those he desires to reach. It is essential to learn the Qur'an and important parts of the Hadith. Then he can communicate sensitively, effectively and intelligently with them.

The second point, which arises out of the first one, is the need *to seek for common ground with Muslims* in their beliefs, especially those which agree with our own beliefs and scriptural teachings. Throughout this book this is the basic principle applied to using the Bible in witnessing to Muslims. Where you can establish common ground, you can gain a better hearing and present the Gospel against the background of what Muslims already believe. Paul did this and you will find much power in witnessing when you do the same. "*What* you worship as unknown, *this* I proclaim to you," Paul declared.

A very fine example of how Jesus himself used this approach is found in his famous conversation with the woman of Samaria. She came every day from the town of Sychar to draw water from Jacob's well which was some distance away from it. Like the other inhabitants she had no choice. Samaria is a semi-desert region and the well was the town's lifeblood. When Jesus spoke to her of his own life-giving powers, he said:

> Every one who drinks of this water will thirst again, but whoever drinks of the water that I shall give him will never thirst, the water that I shall give him will become in him a spring of water welling up to eternal life." *John 4:13-14.*

Jesus spoke right into the context of her immediate presence. She had to come every day to the well to draw water (this very routine testified to the well's limited usefulness), but Jesus could place within her a well of limitless resources which would carry her through to eternal life. Here you can see how well the Gospel can be communicated when it is presented against the background of what the Muslim already believes and the various religious contexts in which you may find him.

There is also a third important lesson we can learn from Paul, this time in his arguments with the Jews in the local synagogues. He argued with them *from the scriptures* (Acts 17:2). He did not resort to illustrations, theological discourses or human reasoning, useful though these may be at times. He based his messages on *the Word of God* which, as we have already seen, is the best foundation for a positive witness. It is the sword of the Spirit, it is living and active, it penetrates the very depths of soul and spirit, and it is God's best instrument for drawing unbelievers to the Gospel of his Son.

A word in closing at this point seems appropriate. Paul placed little, if any, emphasis on creation, culture or his hearer's sensitivities. He worked from the power of his best source, the Word of God, with the Spirit of God as his witness to confirm his message, but he did this in the way the Bible itself does it. Our holy book, as Hebrews says, *pierces to the division of soul and spirit, of joints and marrow*. Primarily the Christian witness is not an attempt to persuade people to believe in the truth of the Gospel, it is, first and foremost, *a call to men and women everywhere to be reconciled to God in their inner beings through faith in Jesus Christ*. The Word of God x-rays the human heart, it analyses our emotions, it challenges our indulgent distractions, it reshapes our hearts and minds, and it confronts the inner man.

Just as we had to confront our own sinfulness and repent of it to become true disciples of Jesus, so Muslims too must come to him in true repentance. It is not simply a shift of allegiance from Muhammad to Jesus. It is also a turning from darkness to light, from self-centredness to Christ-centredness, from spiritual death to eternal life. Ever since the fall of Adam the call of God has been to renewal and a genuine Biblical witness will expose the Muslim heart as well as his mind and redirect him to a living hope in God's perfect Saviour, his Son Jesus Christ.

This theme is also explored consistently in this book. I trust you will find many different ways of effectively witnessing to Muslims and of using the Word of God itself as your basic witness-source in the chapters that follow. With a love for Muslims and the power of God's Word in your hands, you too can be God's own messenger to bring many of them to salvation, the saving grace of God which we know is found in Jesus alone.

John Gilchrist

Benoni, South Africa

12th August 2003

Part One:

Old Testament

Personalities and Prophecies

Adam

The Man of Dust, the Man from Heaven

The Fall of Adam and Eve in the Qur'an

Convincing atheists, humanists, evolutionists, naturalists and agnostics of the authenticity of the Biblical story of Adam and Eve is no easy task, but fortunately in Muslim evangelism the issue is not in dispute. The Qur'an describes both the creation of Adam and Eve as well as their transgression and fall in very similar terms to those found in the Bible and Muslims not only recognise the story but even regard Adam as one of the great prophets of God. The narrative, like so many of the brief biographical records of the Old Testament prophets and patriarchs, is very sketchy in the Qur'an and lacking in detail, but it is sufficient to establish much common ground between Christians and Muslims on the subject.

Adam was created from an *'alaq*, a clot of blood (Surah 96:2), and was taught the nature of all things (Surah 2:31). Both he and his wife Eve were placed in *al-Jannat*, the Garden, and told to eat freely of all the bountiful fruits therein save one tree which they were not to approach lest they ran into harm and wrongdoing (Surah 7:35). When Allah commanded all the angels of heaven to bow down to Adam they did except *Iblis*, the Devil, who refused to do so. When challenged on his disobedience he replied that he would not bow down to a creature moulded from mud and clay (Surah 15:29-33). For this he was cast out of heaven and became *ash-Shaytaan*, Satan the Devil. He then appeared to them to tempt them into sin and unbelief. The narrative continues:

> Then Satan whispered an evil suggestion to them, to show them clearly their shame that had been hidden from them and said "Your Lord has only forbidden you this tree lest you should become angels or such beings as live for ever." And he swore to them both: "Surely I am a sincere adviser to you." Surah 7:20-21.

The Qur'an does not say how Eve was created, nor does it point out that it was Eve alone who was tempted by the devil. The story, however, compares with the Biblical record in all its essentials, however, especially their fall which is recorded in the following passage:

> Then Satan made them slip from it, and caused them to depart from the state they were in. And We said "Get Down, all of you with enmity towards each other. On the earth there will be a dwelling place for you for a time." Surah 2:36

Adam, however, relented towards his Lord who thereafter taught him words of inspiration. The command to "Get down!" is repeated in verse 38 where Allah commands "all of you," meaning the whole human race, to leave the Garden with the promise that when guidance comes from Allah, those who follow it will have nothing to fear. The Qur'an follows the Bible in declaring that Adam and Eve fell by eating of the forbidden tree. Yusuf Ali, the well-known Muslim translator of the Qur'an, says in a footnote to this passage that as the plural of the Arabic word *habata*, meaning to fall down, is used in the verse quoted, "evidently Adam is a type of all mankind" while Mohammed Marmaduke Pickthall, another Muslim translator, says the same: "Here the command is in the plural, as addressed to Adam's race." The word for "all of you" in Surah 2:38 is *jamii'aa*, an Arabic word defined in Kassis' *A Concordance of the Qur'an*, as "a host, a congregation, all, together, altogether" (p.595). Not only, therefore, does the Qur'an clearly teach the fall of Adam but it also, like Bible, implicates the whole human race in his act of disobedience and its consequences.

The root meaning of the word habata is to crash down, to descend, to fall, or to get down. In Surah 2:36 the form used is the imperative, *ihbit* (*ahbituwa* in the text), and means simply "Get out! Descend! Fall down!" The same word is used two verses later in the command to the whole human race to descend with them both. The traditions of Islam teach that the Garden, known in Islam as *al-Jannatul-'Adn*, the Garden of Eden, was in heaven and that Adam and Eve were cast out of Paradise after they had disobeyed God. Both they and their offspring, the whole human race, have since been confined to a temporal, earthly existence where they have all died and been buried. The story of Adam's expulsion from Paradise reads as follows:

> Adam was externed from the Paradise between the *zuhr* (afternoon) and *'dsr* (the declining of day) prayers. His stay in Paradise had been half the day of the next world, and the day there is equal to

> one thousand years based on the calculation made by the people of this world. He was cast down on a mountain in India known as *Nawdh* and Eve was cast at *Juddah*.
>
> *Ibn Sa'd, Kitab al-Tabaqat al-Kabir, Vol.1, p.21*

Despite this similarity with the Biblical record of Adam's sin and fall and the imputation of his transgression to the whole human race, the Qur'an does not pursue the matter further. It thereafter regards sin simply as an act of individual wrongdoing either to be forgiven by Allah or condemned at his pleasure, or to be cancelled out by a good deed. Another passage does, however, strongly emphasise not only the seriousness of the first transgression but also its wider consequences:

> So by deceit he caused them to fall. When they had tasted of the tree their shame was revealed to them and they began to cover themselves with leaves from the Garden. And their Lord called to them: "Did I not forbid you that tree and say to you that Satan is a sworn enemy to you?" They said, "Our Lord! We have wronged our souls. If you do not forgive us or have mercy on us, we will be of the losers." He said, "Get down - with enmity between yourselves. And you will have the earth as your abode and provision for a time." Surah 7:22-24.

It should be obvious that there is tremendous material here for an effective witness to God's saving grace in Jesus Christ, the second Adam, who voluntarily descended from heaven to become man, committed no sin, and reversed the effect of Adam's sin. We shall see how this can be done.

The Biblical account of Adam's Sin and Fall

In the Qur'an it is interesting to note that Satan calls the forbidden tree the "tree of Eternity" (Surah 20:120), another hint to the fact that by disobeying God and eating from it, Adam would implicate the whole of humanity in serious long-term consequences. It is in the Bible, especially the description it gives of the tree, that we obtain a much more comprehensive picture of why God commanded Adam and Eve to leave it alone:

> And the Lord God commanded the man saying, "You may eat freely of every tree of the garden; but of the tree of the knowledge of good and evil you shall not eat, for in the day that you eat of it you shall die." *Genesis 2:16-17*

The tree had to be avoided because it was the tree of "the knowledge of good and evil," meaning that if the ate of it, Adam and Eve would come to know what evil was and its distinction from good. In consequence of this, being partakers of evil, they would be cut off from the tree of life, lose their experience of the life of God in their hearts, and eventually die and return to the ground. Hence, when they did sin, God declared:

> You are dust, and to dust you shall return. *Genesis 3:19*

Muslims really have no knowledge or understanding of what it was about the forbidden tree that made the act of eating its fruit so terribly wrong. The Qur'an gives no explanation other than to declare the tree forbidden, but the Bible does in its description of the tree and in Satan's temptation to Eve when he said:

> You will not die. For God knows that when you eat of it your eyes will be opened, and you will be like God, knowing good and evil.
> *Genesis 3:4-5*

Satan and his angels had fallen because of their desire to be like God, to oppose his authority, and to set themselves up as the masters of their own destiny (Isaiah 14:12-14, 2 Peter 2:4). Now he was tempting Eve, and through her to Adam, to break faith with God and do the same. It was a call to declare independence from God, to refuse to submit to his authority, and to establish their own. When God created Adam he gave him dominion over everything on the earth, in the seas, and over all living creatures (Genesis 1:26). God made man in his own image, in his likeness (Genesis 5:1), meaning that man was able to bear all the attributes of God and reflect his glory. God did not make man already perfected in righteousness but rather in an innocent state with a potential and inclination towards uprightness. "God made man upright" (Ecclesiastes 7:29) and, while putting all things under his feet, only commanded in return that man should be subject to him in his personality, dominion and character.

The tree of the knowledge of good and evil symbolised this sole area where man would not have authority. By not eating of it Adam would acknowledge God's authority over him and that he was called to be a servant of God. Satan's temptation was to shake off God's authority and become gods in their own right, to become "like God" and so determine their own destiny. Adam and Eve did not know that the actual result would be exactly the opposite - that they would fall from their dignity and upright state, lose their relationship with God and the spiritual life surging within them, and become evil like the devil instead. The Qur'an also makes Satan mislead them into believing they would benefit from disobeying God and obtain an exalted status of their own when he promises them they would become like angels or immortal beings (Surah 7:20).

As we will see, it is important to point out to Muslims that the sin of Adam and Eve was not just a transgression. It was a deliberate act of defiance, a renunciation of authority. God's only command was that they should, in their characters, hearts and inner beings, remain subject to him. Instead they fell for Satan's temptation that they could become "like God" and so grasped at equality with God. This was tantamount to shirk, associating themselves as partners with God. It was to arrogate to themselves a complete likeness with him in authority and dominion. Quite simply it was an appalling blasphemy. To the unenlightened the act of eating of the forbidden fruit might seem like no more than a transgression of a simple command. It was not. The tree symbolised God's right to complete authority over man's obligation to be righteous, faithful, obedient, true and devoted to him. By breaking the command not to eat of its fruit, Adam and Eve thoroughly defied God at the root of their beings, disowning his lordship over their lives. The consequences for the human race have been horrendous.

Did Adam Simply Forget His Lord's Command?

Muslims traditionally underrate the effect of that first transgression. They claim Adam merely slipped in a moment of temporary forgetfulness and that, once he had repented of his oversight and asked forgiveness, he was duly forgiven. It is vital to show them that the Qur'an takes a far more serious view of the matter, stating plainly that Satan brought about *their fall* (Surah 7:22) and that Allah deliberately chased them out of the Garden and cast them down to earth where their previous state of peacefulness and felicity would give way to malice and hatred (Surah 7:24). It goes on to appeal to the "Children of Adam" to avoid being seduced by Satan "in the same manner as he got your parents out of the Garden" (Surah 7:27). Their sin was not a single act of transgression that could easily be forgiven as a minor, isolated act of wrongdoing. It was an act of gross rebellion, a total rejection of God's rule over the whole human race, and it had awful consequences.

> Sin came into the world through one man and death through sin, and so death spread to all men because all men sinned.
> *Romans 5:12*

We do not believe that they were cast out of Paradise as the Bible states the Garden was the source of the Tigris and Euphrates rivers on earth (Genesis 2:14). Nonetheless the Muslim belief actually helps to strengthen the effect of their sin. Ask any Muslim if Adam and Eve could have died in heaven, in *Jannat al-Firdaus* (the Garden of Paradise). They will invariably say "no." Also ask them if they would have been cast out of the Garden to a decaying earth if they had not sinned and again the answer will be "no." Lastly, would their offspring have perished in Paradise? Once again you'll get the same answer.

Therefore neither Adam nor Eve, nor any of their billions of offspring, would ever have died had they not broken faith with God and been cast out of Paradise. By implication Islam supports the Biblical teaching that death was the consequence of their sin - firstly, spiritual death and separation from God in the act of rebellion, and then later physical extinction at the end of a temporal life.

Can it really be argued that there was no intention on Adam's part to disobey God and that his transgression was no more than an excusable lapse of memory? The Qur'an shows plainly that Adam and Eve succumbed to Satan's temptation and this despite the fact that Allah had warned them that Satan was an adversary who would seek to get them out of the Garden (Surah 20:117). Adam and Eve must both have had incredibly poor memories to forget God's one command to them and the one consequence they would wished to have avoided. Satan words to Adam, according to the Qur'an, were:

> O Adam! Shall I lead you to the Tree of Eternity and to a kingdom which never decays? *Surah 20:120*

Adam chose to believe Satan and to disobey God. Moreover in Surah 7:20 Satan actually reminded Adam of Allah's command to him not to eat of the forbidden tree. How can one possibly sustain the argument that Adam merely "forgot" his Lord's command, the only negative commandment he ever received and that from God himself? Furthermore, if this was only a minor mistake as Muslims claim, why was the penalty so severe? The whitewashing and diluting of Adam's transgression by Muslims is usually done in the interests of maintaining the hypothesis in traditional

Islam, contradicted by the Qur'an, that all the prophets were sinless. (See the companion volume to this book, *Facing the Muslim Challenge*, pp.46-48). If Adam was a prophet as they believe, then he too could not actually have sinned. Ask any Muslim, then, who it was who introduced sin into the world, when this happened, what the first sin was, and what the effect on the human race was. Obviously there can be no answer based on any sources. The disobedience of Adam was the great single sin that brought the human race into the decaying, sinful world it struggles with today and its ultimate consequence was the worst that could be imagined, death itself.

To be delivered from this shattering consequence the world obviously needs a deliverance from both sin and death. Merely asking God for forgiveness won't help. Even though the Qur'an teaches that Adam and Eve were forgiven (the Bible is silent on the subject), Allah never let them back into the beautiful Garden of Paradise where the Tree of Eternal Life was. Instead they struggled on with the hardships of an earthly existence and eventually died. Obviously a lot more than merely a declaration of forgiveness is needed for the human race to find its way back to Paradise and here is where the Christian witness to the Muslim comes in. Let's see how our common ground on this vital subject can be used as a basis for effective witness to the grace of God as it has been revealed in the Lord Jesus Christ.

The second Adam: Jesus the Universal Redeemer

It is not hard to show Muslims what the effect of Adam's sin was. It had a calamitous effect on the whole human race. Both Adam and Eve were driven from the Garden in which God had placed them. God *drove them out* as both the Bible and the Qur'an clearly state (Genesis 3:24, Surah 20:123). The human race found itself in a world where sin and death reign (Romans 5:21). No one was allowed back into the Garden and no one became as upright as Adam and Eve had been in the beginning. Even Muhammad is recorded in the traditions of Islam as confirming that all human beings were implicated in the original sin and fall:

> Anas reported that it was said by the Messenger of Allah (saw): Every son of Adam is a sinner, and the best of sinners are those who repent consistently. *Sunan Ibn Majah, Vol.5, p.489*

Enter the man Christ Jesus. The Qur'an has an interesting statement about him, linking him to Adam and comparing the two men. It says:

> The likeness of Jesus with Allah is as the likeness of Adam. He created him from dust, then said to him, "Be!" - and he came to be.
> *Surah 3:58*

Muslims are familiar with the catchy Arabic phrase *Kun! faya kun.* The only time the Qur'an compares the two men it says the same about them. Both were created simply by the Word (*kalam*) and Power (*'amr*) of Allah. Muslims see no distinction between them. Yet the Bible is at pains to *distinguish* them and in every place where they are mentioned together the book *contrasts* them. The difference is summed up in this verse:

> For as in Adam all die, so also in Christ shall all be made alive.
> *1 Corinthians 15:21*

The Qur'an appears to be unaware of a much needed solution to the problem caused by Adam's transgression. Sinfulness, decay, enmity and death were the effects of the first man's sin. "Abraham died, as did the prophets," the Jews exclaimed to Jesus (John 8:52), showing that no one had escaped the devastating consequences of the fall. Here we have a tremendous opportunity to show Muslims who Jesus really was and why he came to earth. He was not just an ordinary man, made from the dust as the Qur'an suggests. He *assumed* human form, he was born in the *likeness* of sinful flesh (Romans 8:3), but he, in his soul and spirit, had existed before the world had ever been made (John:1:1-3). He was there when Satan fell like lightning from heaven before Adam and Eve were even created (Luke 10:18). He came down from heaven (John 6:51). He was the only human being without sin (John 8:46, 2 Corinthians 5:21, Hebrews 4:15, 1 Peter 2:25). He has the power of eternal life (John 10:28).

It is important to emphasise to Muslims the total contrast between Jesus and Adam. Adam and Eve had grasped at equality with God and independence from his control but, in doing so, brought themselves and the whole human race down to destruction. Jesus by nature had that equality with God as the eternal Son to the Father, but he voluntarily chose to become totally dependent on his Father as a human being, assumed the form of Adam and Eve, yet was willing to suffer and endure death and humiliation such as they would never have known had they remained faithful to God.

> Have this mind among yourselves, which is yours in Christ Jesus, who, though he was in the form of God, did not count equality with God a thing to be grasped, but emptied himself, taking the form of a servant, being born in the likeness of men. And being found in

> human form he humbled himself and became obedient unto death, even death on a cross. *Philippians 2:5-8*

Adam grasped at higher things beyond his reach. Jesus emptied himself to assume lower things. Adam disobeyed God even though he only had to remain obedient to God to live forever. Jesus obeyed God completely, yet gave up his life to become our Saviour. He became obedient *to death*, even to death *on a cross*. Here was perfect obedience.

> Although he was a Son, he learnt obedience through what he suffered; and being made perfect, he became the source of eternal salvation to all who obey him. *Hebrews 5:8-9*

Jesus was the only man who lived in absolute, perfect conformity to God's will. He always did what was pleasing to the Father (John 8:29). He knew that, no matter how low his estate on earth, a humble man without possessions from an insignificant family in Nazareth from which no good thing could surely come (John 1:46), there was nothing more glorious than that he should be under God's holy and gracious will. Adam and Eve returned to the dust. Jesus, however, rose from the dead. Because of his perfect love and obedience God glorified him as Lord of all.

> Therefore God has highly exalted him and bestowed on him the name which is above every name, that at the name of Jesus every knee should bow, in heaven and on earth and under the earth, and every tongue confess that Jesus Christ is Lord, to the glory of God the Father. Philippians 2:9-11.

In witnessing to Muslims we have a wonderful opportunity to show how the whole human race is represented in two heads, Adam and Christ. The sin of the one man Adam brought the whole human race down to sin and death. The perfect obedience of Jesus, however, and his saving death and resurrection, can bring all men back to the path to eternal life. As Muslims believe that Adam and Eve were created in heaven but fell to earth when they sinned and died here, so Jesus was born on earth but rose to heaven where he stands alone at the right hand side of God. We do not believe Adam and Eve were created in heaven but the contrast between them in Muslim belief needs to emphasised. Muslims accept that Jesus was taken to heaven.

According to Islam Jesus is the only person who is not buried on earth but is physically alive in heaven. While more than five billion people live on earth and many more billions have lived and died before us, right now just one man, only one, is alive in heaven and that is Jesus Christ. *He alone has gone back into the presence of God and the realm of Paradise from which Adam and Eve were driven out*. Jesus, by dying for us, reversed the effect of Adam's sin. He has the power of eternal life and gives it to all who believe in him. Emphasise with Muslims this one great contrast: as *one man* brought us into sin and condemnation, so *another man* delivers us from it. The Bible contrasts the effect of Adam's sin with the effect of Jesus' deliverance from it in these words:

> But the free gift is not like the trespass. For if many died through one man's trespass, much more have the grace of God and the free gift of that grace of that one man Jesus Christ abounded for many. And the free gift is not like the effect of that one man's sin. For the judgment following one trespass brought condemnation, but the free gift following many trespasses brings justification.
>
> *Romans 5:15-16*

> If because of one man's trespass, death reigned through that one man, much more will those who receive the abundance of grace and the free gift of righteousness reign in life through the one man Jesus Christ. *Romans 5:17*

We need to concentrate on this great contrast just as intensely as the Bible does. Death was the consequence of Adam's sin. Muslims cannot deny this. There is no death in Paradise, only here on this earth to which Adam and Eve were driven and where every living thing must die eventually. Yet it was on this same earth that Jesus, who laid down his life which no one could take from him (John 10:17) and, by rising from the dead, becomes the source of eternal life to all who follow him.

> Then as one man's trespass led to condemnation for all men, so one man's act of righteousness leads to acquittal and life for all men. For as by one man's disobedience many were made sinners, so by one man's obedience many will be made righteous.
>
> *Romans 5:18-19*

Adam was made from the dust and returned to it. Jesus, however, came from heaven and returned where *he* had come from. All who have sinned in Adam will die like Adam did. All who believe in Jesus will be raised from the dead to live for ever in the eternal heavenly kingdom to come at the end of time. As opposed to the Qur'anic claim that Adam and Jesus were exactly the same, the Bible says:

> Thus it is written, "The first man Adam became a living being"; the last Adam became a life-giving Spirit. But it is not the spiritual which is first but the physical, and then the spiritual. The *first* man was from the *earth*, a *man of dust*; the *second* man is from *heaven*. As was the man of dust, so are those who are of the dust, and as is the man of heaven, so are those who are of heaven. Just as we have borne the image of the man of dust, we shall also bear the image of the man of heaven. *1 Corinthians 15:45-49*

The contrast could not be put more emphatically. Christians, in witness to Muslims, need to emphasise the seriousness of sin. Islam takes too light a view of its devastating power, hardly recognising that death is its final and complete consequence. Yet, by narrating the fall of Adam and Eve in terms similar to those we find in the Bible, the Qur'an does give us common ground, a platform with which to show Muslims what the effects of sin really are and why a Saviour from heaven was needed.

Jesus rose from the dead and, through the Holy Spirit, releases into his followers a life-giving power that already has passed through the grip of death and assures us of salvation. As Adam died, so we will die. But as Jesus rose from the dead and ascended to heaven, so we will do the same. Muhammad lies dead and buried in Medina. Adam lies dead and buried somewhere. The likeness of Muhammad is the same as the likeness of Adam. He lies in the dust, unlike Jesus who lives in glory in heaven and is able to save all Muslims and fill them with his resurrection life-giving power as well.

Eve

Satan's Three Great Temptations

Do Muslims have an awareness of sinfulness?

The Bible does not regard wrongdoing as simply the act of committing a sin against God which can be cancelled out by a good deed, nor does it regard human beings as having the freedom, from a neutral position, to choose between good and evil. As we have seen, it regards all of humankind, since the sin of the first man Adam, as being under the power of sin and needing an act of redemption to restore its relationship with God. Original Sin is the name or title given to this definition, meaning that all the sons of Adam are in a state of sinfulness, with a tendency to evil, as slaves to sin and bound to do its bidding (John 8:34), with a deadening effect on the soul (Ephesians 2:1) resulting in the eventual death of the body.

Islam does not take the effect of sin to such extremes. It regards wrongdoing as a very serious matter but does not teach that all men and women are held in sin's destructive, deadly grip and cannot be forgiven or saved unless God himself activates a redeeming work from his side to remedy the situation. The Qur'an does teach that there is an enmity between God and man and that sin and wrongdoing have had a devastating effect on the human race. "Indeed man is in ruin", it declares (Surah 103:3) and to some extent it confirms the Biblical concept of sinfulness in this verse::

> I do not claim that my soul is innocent for man is prone to evil.
> *Surah 12:53*

Yet Muslims scholars have always taught that sins are no more than acts of wrongdoing, breaches of the laws of Islam, which can be remedied by good deeds, repentance and the forgiveness of Allah. Sinfulness, as a state of the soul motivating mankind instinctively towards evil, does not come into the Islamic equation. The Qur'an uses two words which are usually translated simply as "sin," namely *dhanb* and *khati'ah*, and also often uses the word *dhulm* meaning "wrong." To these scholars, once a man professes Islam and lives as a Muslim, all evil deeds, thoughts and words are only transgressions of the law to be punished or forgiven. Sure, the enemies of Allah are said to have a sickness in their hearts (Surah 8:49), but this is not a state of sinfulness but rather an attitude of ill-will towards Muslim believers with the intention of misleading and beguiling them away from Islam.

Muslims have traditionally distinguished between two types of sin, *kabirah* - the "great" sins, and *saghirah* - the "little" sins. The first are serious misdemeanours which, if not repented of, will lead to punishment, and the second are venial errors which are common to all believers and will be forgiven more easily. The Hadith records teach that Muhammad regarded seven sins as more heinous than all others, as in this text:

> Abu Hurairah reported the Apostle of Allah (saw) as saying: Refrain from seven (sins) which cause destruction. He was asked, What are they, Apostle of Allah? He replied: To assign a partner to Allah, magic, to kill a soul (man) which is prohibited by Allah except for which is due, to take usury, to consume the property of an orphan, to retreat on the day of battle, and to slander chaste women, indiscreet but believing.
>
> *Sunan Abu Dawud, Vol.2, p.809*

Other records in the Hadith show that, in Islam, acts of wrongdoing can be compensated or expiated by acts of repentance, good deeds, righteous works and enduring the legal punishments prescribed by Islamic law. This tradition is typical of those that regard sin in Islam as no more than wilful acts of wrongdoing rather than evidences of a sinful heart in need of redemption:

> Narrated 'Ubada bin As-Samit: I gave the pledge of allegiance to the Prophet (saw) with a group of people and he said, "I take your pledge that you will not worship anything besides Allah, will not steal, will not commit infanticide, will not slander others by forging false statements and spreading it, and will not disobey me in anything good. And whoever among you fulfils all these, his reward is with Allah. And whoever commits any of the above crimes and received his legal punishment in this world, that will be his expiation and purification. But if Allah screens his sin, it will be up to Allah, Who will either punish or forgive him according to his wish".
>
> *Sahih al-Bukhari, Vol.8, p.518*

In the light of all these teachings you would not expect Muslims to have an awareness of sinfulness, yet it has been my experience that most of them do. I have often been impressed with their consciousness, which they freely express, that a tendency to sin resides deep within their souls. When challenged about their lives, they will openly admit that sin is so prevalent that at times they may not even be aware of it. "You know, there are so many times when we sin we don't even realise we are doing it. We don't always know what is wrong and what isn't." How often I have heard that kind of statement.

Often it runs deeper. Addiction to habits, such as smoking, swearing, abusiveness and the like, make them aware of a bondage to sin from within their beings that is not easy to overcome. When I have challenged them about their sins, they regularly reply "Oh, but we know Allah is forgiving and we pray to him and trust he will forgive us. You must just determine not to commit that sin again." I have then asked: "But all wrongdoing is sin. Why simply declare that you will not commit one specific sin again? What about all the others?" Sure, they agree, you have to repent of all sins. Then I have asked the key question: "If you know sinning is wrong and that you are disobeying the laws of God, why don't you wake up tomorrow morning and, before doing anything else, pray to God and say you know all sins are wrong, so from this moment on you'll never sin again for the rest of your life."

Without exception the response has always been the same. "That's impossible! No one can proclaim to God that he will never sin again. You can't make a promise like that for even one day, never mind a lifetime. Often you're sinning without even knowing it." Yes, Muslims have a very definite awareness of their own sinfulness. The reason is simple - the Biblical assessment of sin and its effect on human nature is the correct one. Whatever the Qur'an, the Hadith or Muslim scholars may teach, human sinfulness and the tendency to evil are inherently part of every man's nature. Many a Muslim painfully knows the meaning of these words:

> The heart is deceitful above all things, and desperately corrupt; who can understand it? I the Lord search the mind and try the heart, to give to every man according to his ways, according to the fruit of his doings. *Jeremiah 17:9-10*

It has often been said that sin has created a Christ-shaped vacuum in every man's heart. This is absolutely true and, no matter what a Muslim may be taught to believe about himself, it's true of him too. Only Jesus

Christ can fill the dark void in the depths of the heart caused by the devastating effect of human sinfulness. Only the Spirit of Christ can enliven any soul dead in its trespasses and sins.

Here is an area where any Christian can witness effectively to Muslims of God's saving grace in Jesus Christ. In the last chapter we saw how to impress on Muslims that the first transgression of Adam and Eve had devastating consequences. Here, by drawing them out on the inner motives, passions, jealousies, angers, lusts, unholy desires and evil promptings that surge from the depths of their being, a Christian can show them how God has resolved this problem and how, by believing in Jesus who died to deliver us not only from the guilt of sin but also its power, they can be reconciled to God and be given fulness of life in receiving the Holy Spirit.

There is one very important comparison in the Bible that can be raised in this context and used to emphasise just who Jesus was, how he conquered the power of sin, and how he can deliver any man from its deadly effects.

Eve's Capitulation to Satan's Threefold Temptation

Only one woman is named in the Qur'an, Mary the mother of Jesus. Eve (named Hawwa in Islam) is mentioned simply as the wife of Adam (Surah 2:35, 7:19), and no mention is made of the fact that Satan first tempted her before she persuaded her husband to eat of the forbidden fruit. In the Qur'an Satan tempts them both at the same time, whispering suggestions and swearing he was their sincere adviser (Surah 7:20-21). Muslims, generally, do not object to the Biblical record of their fall, however, and it is very useful to analyse the true nature of the devil's temptation. We read:

> So when the woman saw that the tree was good for food, and that it was a delight to the eyes, and that the tree was desired to make one wise, she took of its food and ate; and she also gave some to her husband, and he ate. *Genesis 3:6*

It was not just a simple enticement to eat the fruit. It was a comprehensive temptation directed at the core of her being and, as the passage shows, had a threefold character. Firstly, Eve saw that the tree was "good for food." This meant it was obviously tasty, in good shape and would benefit her physical body if she ate of it. There was nothing wrong with the fruit itself. It had no worms! Satan succeeded in misleading her because he got her to focus on the fruit itself rather than the God who had simply forbidden her to eat of it.

Muslims are aware that many temptations to sin cause them to fall simply because the action itself does not appear to carry negative consequences. The end result often appears profitable as long as the declared will of God is ignored. Pornography, drug-taking, financial corruption in business and sexual immorality can all be very appetising and seem harmless as long as no one else knows what you are doing. It's only when they lead to rape, indecent assault, AIDS, criminal prosecution, job losses, drug addiction, venereal diseases, divorce and other unwanted consequences that the wrongdoing becomes apparent for what it really is. All these come from desires for immediate physical gratification and there is not a Muslim in the world that does not know this level of temptation.

Secondly, Eve saw the food was "a delight to the eyes." God had said "do not touch it," but Eve, disregarding the commandment again, judged the fruit purely by its appearance. It looked good. There was nothing obviously wrong with it. In fact, once you looked at it closely, it appeared to be an object of great beauty. Her sin did not consist in choosing to pick and eat an object which was inedible or poisonous, it was in simply defying the will of her Creator who had commanded her not to eat it. Once again, by disrespecting His will and asserting her own, she fell. Many a Muslim knows the outcome of focusing on the beauty of something lawfully beyond his reach - another man's wife, a luxury car he cannot afford, an X-rated TV program he shouldn't watch - and falling for its beauty without recognising the identity of the devil persuading him to pursue it.

Thirdly, Eve perceived that the food was "to be desired to make one wise." She believed Satan when he suggested that, by taking it, she would become "like God, knowing good and evil" (Genesis 3:5). She was fooled into thinking she would advance her status and become like the deity himself, not recognising the perfidy of the one who spoke to her. Instead she fell and became like the devil, knowing the power and presence of evil. Muslims know the meaning of the proverb "Pride comes before a fall." History, both Muslim and non-Muslim, testifies to the ultimate end of all power-mad rulers who pursue their arrogant ambitions and seek to become their own gods over the people they control.

There's a verse in the New Testament that defines this threefold temptation as emphatically and clearly as it could possibly be put. It is:

> For all that is in the world, the lust of the flesh and the lust of the eyes and the pride of life, is not of the Father but of the world.
> *1 John 2:16*

The "lust of the flesh" made Eve see that the tree was good for food, the "lust of the eye" that it was attractive to the sight, and "the pride of life" that it was to be desired to make one wise. Built into one temptation were evil characteristics that she had formerly never known or even thought possible - greed, covetousness, pride, arrogance, selfishness, shame and dishonour - and in the centuries to come these were to grow to enormous proportions in the billions of her offspring who would choose to listen to the devil rather than the God of all the Universe. One awful, comprehensive temptation fully absorbing all three of the desires John mentions, brought about the downfall of the human race.

By identifying these three causes of all sinful actions, the Christian can witness very effectively to Muslims of God's saving grace in Jesus Christ. We turn to a time when the devil, up to the same tricks, tried the same threefold temptation on him.

The Obedience of the One Man Jesus Christ

The Qur'an does not mention a very important promise God made shortly after Adam and Eve had eaten of the forbidden fruit. He said to Satan:

> I will put enmity between you and the woman, and between your seed and her seed; he shall bruise your head, and you shall bruise his heel. *Genesis 3:15*

He promised that one of her offspring, just one, would rise in an age to come who would not be affected by their fall, who would not be like the devil but would in fact be his sworn and mortal enemy. He would be on God's side and, though bruised in the conflict, would conquer Satan and eventually destroy him. The man was Jesus Christ and Satan recognised him. For the first thirty years he grew up and lived an ordinary life as a carpenter's son in Nazareth, a humble village. His neighbours, during this time, saw nothing unusual about him (Mark 6:2-3). Satan, however, marked him - especially what he noticed and that was that he was the first and only man to live on earth without sin in complete obedience to God (1 Peter 2:22-23).

Jesus finally came into the open when he was baptised by John and the Spirit of God descended on him in bodily form, as a dove (Matthew

3:16). Immediately afterwards, just as God had driven Adam and Eve from the Garden into a decaying world full of thorns, so Jesus was driven away from his normal countryside into the wilderness (Mark 1:12). There he fasted forty days and nights. Satan must have wondered at his purpose but, despite not being able to identify it, did perceive that, at the end of the forty days, Jesus was about as weak as a human being could be. Hunger strikers usually die after about sixty-five days and after forty days are almost at the point of no return. Satan knew his best chance of catching Jesus in a moment of complete physical weakness, when he had no natural strength to resist him, was right now.

There is so much to compare between the three temptations that followed and the similar temptation to Eve. Here is a wonderful opportunity to show Muslims how Jesus resisted temptation to sin at its fullest intensity, how he conquered the power of sin, and how he can be our strength today. There are no parallels in the life of Muhammad. The first temptation of the devil went like this:

> If you are the Son of God, command this stone to become bread.
>
> *Luke 4:3*

There was a vast difference between this temptation and the one Eve had faced. She was in a beautiful garden, Jesus was in a barren desert. She had ample access to all the food she could possibly desire, Jesus had none and had not eaten for forty days. He was emaciated with hunger. It was as if Satan was mocking him. "You are supposed to be the Son of God, yet here you perish with hunger. Look how your Father treats you. He has made you the hungriest and weakest man on all the earth. Now, if you will just listen to me, I'll show you how to save yourself. Turn these stones into loaves of bread."

The fruit Eve ate was a delicacy, good for food and delight to the eyes. Jesus desperately needed just a piece of staple diet, a loaf of bread, to survive. Satan offered Jesus the Midas touch, as it were, yet Jesus resisted him, saying "Man shall not live by bread alone" (Luke 4:4). He stood by his commitment to live by every word of God, no matter where it might lead him.

The contrast between Eve and Jesus is striking - two extremes, to be precise. She had no need to eat but did. He desperately needed food but declined to use his powers against his Father's will to satisfy himself. At his weakest he resisted the temptation to indulge the "lust of the flesh" at its fullest extent and intensity. So Satan tried his second temptation, showing him all the kingdoms of the world in a moment of time, and saying:

> To you I will give all this authority and their glory; for it has been delivered to me, and I give it to whom I will. If you, then, will worship me, it shall all be yours. *Luke 4:6-7*

Again Jesus resisted the temptation, saying to Satan "You shall worship the Lord your God, and him only shall you serve" (Luke 4:8). This time Satan attempted to make Jesus fall through the "lust of the eye," dazzling his vision with a display of all the kingdoms of the earth. Once again it was as if he was mocking Jesus, saying "Your Father has also made you the poorest man on earth in this wilderness. You have nothing you can call your own. But if you will listen to me, I will make you the richest man on earth. I'll show you how to use your powers to possess everything on earth for yourself. Just listen to me and, like Eve, ignore the will of your Father."

Again there is a marked contrast between Eve and Jesus. She fell for a piece of fruit - Jesus resisted an offer to obtain the whole world. When Eve ate the fruit sin, and human sinfulness, had only just begun to affect mankind. It had only just been conceived. In the fulness of time, however, when Jesus appeared on earth, it had reached its pitch. The Bible shows how sin grows to maturity in these words:

> Then desire when it has conceived gives birth to sin; and sin when it is full-grown brings forth death. *James 1:15*

By Jesus' time the emperors or Rome, such as Julius and Augustus Caesar, were seeking to gain the whole world for themselves. Others like Alexander the Great had also attempted this before them. "They are only men, you are the Son of God. Use your divine powers to fulfil your own desires and you can do it," Satan was saying to Jesus. Once again sin and temptation had come a long way, from one extreme to the other. Jesus resisted the temptation to indulge the lust of his eyes to its fullest possible extent. So Satan tried his third and last temptation:

> If you are the Son of God, throw yourself down from here; for it is written, "He will give his angels charge over you to guard you," and "On their hands they will bear you up, lest you strike your foot against a stone." *Luke 4:9-11*

For the third time Jesus resisted, saying "It is said, You shall not tempt the Lord your God" (Luke 4:12). This was the temptation to "the pride of life." This time Satan was saying to him "On top of it all, your Father has made you the loneliest man on earth. No one knows where you are, no one cares. If you died, who would be concerned? You are the hungriest, poorest and loneliest man on earth, a travesty of humanity. Now, if you will only listen to me, I will show you how to become the greatest and most popular man who ever lived. I will give you the obedience of the nations."

Eve fell for a temptation just to become wiser, Jesus resisted a temptation to become the greatest man on all the earth. Once again sin had been taken to its fullest extremes, and Jesus resisted it at its greatest extent. Roman rulers, not content to possess everything on earth, were also endeavouring to force their subjects to honour them as divine rulers. Sin had indeed become full-grown.

The method Satan used here to tempt Jesus can be likened to the Hajj Pilgrimage in Islam. Every year hundreds of thousands of Muslim pilgrims come to Mecca from all over the world to encircle the Ka'aba seven times. In 1979 a group of rebels occupied the mosque precincts, declaring one of their number to be the long-awaited Imam Mehdi, a Messianic figure anticipated by Shiah Muslims as well as many Sunnis. The coup failed, however, and the surviving rebels were beheaded in public disgrace. If, however, the pretender had declared "I am Imam Mehdi and to prove it I will jump off the Ka'aba and you will see God's angels come down to protect me" and had accomplished this with a visible rescue by a host of angels from heaven, I have little doubt they would have all been persuaded!

Jesus was tempted by Satan in the same way. The devil gave him a vision of monotheistic believers from all over the earth gathered to worship at God's holy house and tempted him to win their allegiance by a public display of his divine authority. That such a temptation could come from Satan is indicative of the corrupt allegiance of the Jewish nation to the God of Israel at the time. Very significantly, when Jesus did finally come to the Temple, he did the opposite of what Satan had suggested and drove all the moneychangers and pigeon-sellers out of the Temple, making himself most unpopular in the process (John 2:15-20).

The comparisons and contrasts between the three forms of temptation are obvious. What's more, Eve faced only one temptation which embedded all three desires. Jesus faced three separate temptations, stretched to their fullest possible range and magnitude, and effectively resisted them all. In all three cases Satan tempted him as he had baited Adam and Eve - to assert himself independently of his Father's will. He returned to his people and, having conquered the power of sin, prepared himself to conquer its guilt at the cross and so complete the work of redemption. He had bruised the head of Satan. He had "condemned sin in the flesh" (Romans 8:3) he had triumphed over it in its chosen lair, the human body, the source of all sin and wrongdoing. He had discerned the implication of Satan's command "Throw yourself down" (Luke 4:9). He knew this was all men would ever do by heeding his suggestions.

Christians here have a powerful basis to witness to Muslims aware of their own sinfulness. Jesus said the Holy Spirit would come to convict the world of sin (John 16:8) and, by praying for Muslims and witnessing to them, Christians can depend on the Spirit working with them to open the hearts of Muslims to see the degree of their own sinfulness and their need of redemption. Jesus dealt with sin once for all in the wilderness and at the cross. He now releases the power to all his followers to overcome its force and effects as well.

> For the law of the Spirit of life in Christ Jesus has set me free from the law of sin and death. *Romans 8:3*

Many Muslims, having like Pilgrim in John Bunyan's Pilgrim's Progress, become aware of the burden of their sins and the inner controlling sinfulness of their hearts, seek more than a religion, book or way of life to deliver them. Christians, here, are well-equipped to lead them to the Saviour of the world, the Lord Jesus Christ.

Noah

The First Herald of Righteousness

The Construction of the Ark

One of the major themes of the Old Testament is the foreshadowing of the life, death and resurrection of Jesus Christ in many of the great events it records. This is one of the most impressive proofs God has given of the authenticity of the new covenant and that it is the sole means of salvation for all men in all ages. God has sealed the testimony of the Christian Gospels by giving clear indications of the coming work of Jesus in the lives and experiences of the former prophets. So many of them are types of Christ and these types can be used very effectively to show Muslims that all the promises and purposes of God were destined to find their fulfilment in him.

Significantly, none of these prophets typified each other but all of them pointed to the coming of God's Saviour and the redemption he would achieve. As the Qur'an names most of the prominent Old Testament prophets and generally repeats the stories in which the typology is found, Christians have tremendous common ground from which to show Muslims that everything that happened in those days was building towards an awesome climax in Jesus rather than a re-affirmation of it all in the prophet of Islam.

Noah was the first type of Christ. You do not have to read more than three pages of the Bible before he appears. After the fall of Adam and Eve, the human race steadily fell into great wickedness and, contrary to God's hopes and wishes, turned away from and against him. Its rejection of God was emphatic and universal and is summed up in these words:

> The Lord saw that the wickedness of man was great in the earth, and that every imagination of the thoughts of his heart was only evil continually. *Genesis 6:5*

The emphasis in this verse must not be lost: "*every* imagination of the thoughts of his heart was *only evil continually.*" The human race had fallen into a state of complete separation from God. Paul's combination of quotations from the Old Testament in the following passage makes the same point:

> None is righteous, not, not one. No one understands, no one seeks for God. All have turned aside, together they have gone wrong. No one does good, not even one. *Romans 3:10-12*

Genesis goes on to say that the Lord was grieved to his heart and regretted creating man. He wasted no time in deciding to blot the human race out together with all living creatures on the surface of the earth for he was sorry that he had made them. Yet there was one ray of hope, one exception, which was to become the first symbol of God's ultimate purpose to provide a salvation and redemption for mankind. We read:

> But Noah found favour in the eyes of the Lord.
> *Genesis 6:8*

This is not the first mention of the great patriarch in the narrative. When Adam and Eve were cast out of the Garden of Eden they were told:

> Cursed is the ground because of you; in toil you shall eat of it all the days of your life; thorns and thistles it shall bring forth to you; and you shall eat the plants of the field. In the sweat of your face you shall eat bread till you return to the ground, for out of it you were taken; you are dust, and to dust you shall return.
> *Genesis 3:17-19*

Men and women lived much longer then than they do now, yet the effect of the fall and the toil and sweat they were offered (almost in Churchillian fashion: "I can offer you nothing but blood, toil, tears and sweat") was painfully felt. When Lamech reached the age of a hundred and eighty-two, he became the father of a son and called his name Noah, saying:

> Out of the ground which the Lord has cursed this one shall bring us relief from our work and from the toil of our hands.
> *Genesis 5:29*

The very name Noah means rest or relief and Noah's birth symbolised a struggling world's desperate need of a Reliever. Because of its rejection of God, however, the relief was to come to Noah's descendants and not to the masses alive at the time. Noah became a figurehead because he was the only God-fearing man on earth and the first herald of righteousness (2 Peter 2:5). Again the Bible says:

> Noah was a righteous man, blameless in his generation; Noah walked with God. *Genesis 6:9*

The first sign that God's ultimate purpose is not to save the whole human race but only those who form the household of his Saviour Jesus Christ, their figurehead, is found in God's command to Noah. Having warned him that he was about to make an end of all flesh because the earth was filled with violence and wickedness, he commanded him to build an ark, giving him express directions how to build it, for the saving of his household. More expressly, God said to him:

> But I will establish my covenant with you; and you shall come into the ark, you, your sons, your wife, and your son's wives with you.
> *Genesis 6:18*

What happened next is important, because it typifies the saving work of Jesus Christ. God told Noah he would destroy the world through a great flood but, while he was patiently constructing the ark, not a drop of rain fell. As long as it was incomplete nothing changed. So it is with the Church today. God has warned of a second judgment to come:

> By the word of God ... the world that then existed was deluged with water and perished. But by the same word the heavens and earth that now exist have been stored up for fire, being kept until the day of judgment and destruction of ungodly men.
> *2 Peter 3:5-7*

While Jesus is still drawing out men and women to himself, the judgment will not come. So with Noah, while he was still putting the finishing touches on the ark for the saving of his household, there was no sign of the flood to come. This was a momentous task - the ark was the size of a large building. Not only was he preserving human life but was also redeeming a host of birds, animals and reptiles. In the same way when Jesus comes he will not only raise all his own followers to glory but will also ensure that the whole creation will "be set free from its bondage to decay and obtain the glorious liberty of the children of God" (Romans 8:21).

Piece by piece, nail by nail, plank by plank, the ark came together. In the same way man by man, woman by woman, believer by believer, repentant sinner by repentant sinner, the redeemed people of God in Jesus Christ are also coming together. As Noah built God's ark, so Jesus too builds a redeemed household for God (Hebrews 3:3). The typology goes further. We do not know how the crowds reacted to Noah's apparently senseless venture in building such a large ark high up on dry ground, but the Qur'an makes an interesting statement at this point:

> And he began to make the ark (*fulk*). And whenever the chiefs of his people passed by him, they laughed at him.
>
> *Surah 11:38*

This has a remarkable parallel in the life of Jesus. As he hung on the cross and completed his saving work for the household of God, just as Noah had toiled in the construction of his ark, the same thing happened:

> So also the chief priests, with the elders and scribes, mocked him, saying, "He saved others, he cannot save himself."
>
> *Matthew 27:41-42*

Although the parallel is not found in the Bible, its presence in the Qur'an can effectively be used to show how similar the works of Noah and Jesus were at this point. Noah's building of a great ship must have seemed like an exercise in absurdity to his people and it is highly likely that they ridiculed him mercilessly. So also, when Jesus hung on the cross his dying agonies hardly seemed to indicate that the greatest success story in all human history was just moments from being accomplished.

The Great Flood - Salvation for some , Judgement for the rest

For forty days a relentless flood covered the whole earth and every living creature was destroyed. The highest mountains were covered by the waters and they prevailed on the earth for one hundred and fifty days. What God did is summarised in this verse:

> He blotted out every living thing that was upon the face of the ground, man and animals and creeping things and birds of the air; they were blotted out from the earth. Only Noah was left, and those that were with him in the ark. *Genesis 7:23*

What must not be missed is the *contrast* between the effect of the waters on Noah's ark, on the one hand, and the whole earth below. They drowned and destroyed every living creature on the ground but, as the waters increased, they "bore up the ark, and it rose high above the earth" (Genesis 7:17). The ark was *lifted* up with the waters and towered high above the land. So when Jesus returns, although the masses of unbelieving, ungodly sinners will be judged and thrown into the lake of fire, "the dead in Christ will rise first; then we who are alive, who are left, shall be caught up together with them in the clouds to meet the Lord in the air; and so we shall always be with the Lord" (1 Thessalonians 4:16-17). The destruction of the world will be accompanied by the lifting up of the saved, just as it was at the time of the flood.

The story of Noah and the flood is, like so many others we will consider in this book, a wonderful base for witnessing meaningfully to Muslims of God's grace in Christ. Muslims generally love to hear stories, especially those of the ancient prophets which are set out in the Qur'an, and without having the preach at them any Christian can, through comparing the Biblical and Quranic narratives, show how the Gospel was prefigured in the events of past ages. Jesus often spoke in parables to make his points more emphatically and, in the same way, you can share the Gospel with Muslims more effectively by showing how it was prefigured in events like the great flood.

> He did not spare the ancient world, but preserved Noah, a herald of righteousness, with seven other persons, when he brought a flood upon the world of the ungodly. *2 Peter 2:5*

So God will likewise not spare the wicked when Jesus returns but will raise up the followers of Jesus to be heirs of God and fellow-heirs with Christ to be glorified with him (Romans 8:17). Jesus put it in these words:

> When the Son of man comes in his glory, and all the angels with him, then he will sit on his glorious throne. Before him will be gathered all the nations, and he will separate them one from another as a shepherd separates the sheep from the goats, and he will place the sheep at his right hand, but the goats at the left. ... And they will go away into eternal punishment, but the righteous into eternal life.
> *Matthew 25:32-33,46*

Noah became a Saviour through the ark which he built with his toil and labour, so Jesus became the Saviour of the world through his death on the cross. Noah, as his name implies, gave "rest" and "relief" to his household. So Jesus gives eternal rest to all who believe in him.

> By faith Noah, being warned by God concerning events as yet unseen, took heed and constructed an ark for the saving of his household; by this he condemned the world and became an heir of the righteousness which comes by faith.
>
> *Hebrews 11:7*

Typical Similarities between Noah and Jesus

The comparisons between Jesus and Noah go much further and there are many other obvious points where the typology continues. You can use so many of them in showing how Noah was a type of Christ. Ten come to mind and they follow.

1. Noah and Jesus were rejected by their people

The Qur'an states that, despite his passionate appeals to them to accept the messages God was giving him, Noah's people flatly rejected him (Surah 10:73) and called him a liar (Surah 7:64). So also the Bible says of Jesus:

> He came to his own home, and his own people received him not.
>
> *John 1:11*

2. Both Jesus and Noah were accused of being possessed

As already mentioned the Bible does not mention the reaction of the masses to Noah's construction of a huge ark but the Qur'an does and it adds this statement:

> Before them the people of Noah rejected - they rejected our servant and said he was possessed, and drove him away.
>
> *Surah 54:9*

The word for "possessed" here is *majnun*, a word generally meaning crazed or mad. It was commonly used of poets in the time of Muhammad and, when he received the first portion of the Qur'an in what he said was a vision of a strange being in the sky, he came down and, sweating, cried to his wife Khadija to cover him with a mantle as he feared he too was becoming *majnun* like the eccentric poets around Mecca. Interestingly the Arabic word *jinn*, meaning a demon, comes from the same root letters. Jesus was also accused of being possessed by his opponents:

> Are we not right in saying that you are a Samaritan and have a demon? *John 8:48*

> He has a demon, and he is mad; why listen to him? *John 10:20*

3. They both sought the forgiveness of their opponents

Once again, according to the Qur'an, Noah engaged in intense discussions and arguments with his people and called to them, saying "Ask forgiveness of your Lord, for he is ever-forgiving" (Surah 71:10). On the cross Jesus prayed these words:

> Father, forgive them, for they know not what they do. *Luke 23:34*

The Qur'an does go on to say that, when they disobeyed him and persuaded all around to hold to their idols Wadd, Suwa, Yaghuth, Ya'uq and Nasr, Noah changed and prayed to God to leave none of the unbelievers alive on earth. Instead he prayed earnestly for his own forgiveness and the forgiveness of his believing household (Surah 71:21-28).

4. Both Jesus and Noah were rejected as ordinary mortals

The Qur'an has numerous passages outlining the debates between Noah and his people prior to the flood. Once again there are no parallels in the Bible but you can use these Quranic passages to show how similar Noah and Jesus were in support of proofs that Noah was a type of the coming Saviour. This passage in the Qur'an about Noah is interesting as it is very similar to a passage in the Bible about Jesus:

> But the chiefs of his people who disbelieved said: We see you as only a mortal like us, and we note that only the meanest of us are your followers. Nor do you appear to be superior to us in any way. We consider you all to be liars. *Surah 11:27*

Familiarity breeds contempt, so the saying goes, and much the same was said about Jesus' and his family by his kinsmen in this passage:

> Many who heard him were astonished, saying "Where did this man get all this? What is the wisdom given to him? What mighty works are wrought by his hands! Is not this the carpenter, the son of Mary and brother of James and Joses and Judas and Simon, and are not his sisters here with us?" And they took offense at him. *Mark 6:2-3*

5. Their works were to be a sign for all peoples

Noah's sweat and toil in building the ark, in which he was soon to be shut away until the storms had passed, and his ultimate deliverance onto a refreshed earth is a type and symbol of Jesus' suffering on the cross, being shut away in a tomb, and resurrection from the dead three days later. Here again you can use the Qur'an to make the point. This verse is significant:

> So We delivered him and the inmates of the ark, and made it a sign to the nations. *Surah 29:15*

Jesus likewise gave the Sign of Jonah - his internment in a tomb for three days and deliverance therefrom - as a sign for his generation (Matthew 12:39).

6. They were the symbols of righteousness for their age

The quotations from the Qur'an are useful to draw comparisons with Muslims between Noah and Jesus from their own text book, but the most effective parallels come from the Bible. We have already read that, in contrast to all other men on earth who were filled with wickedness and violence, Noah "was a righteous man, blameless in his generation" (Genesis 6:9). So, in contrast to the Jewish leaders whom he had all convicted of sin in the presence of an adulterous woman (John 8:7-9), Jesus could say "Which of you convicts me of sin? If I tell the truth, why do you not believe me?" (John 8:46).

7. Both were given authority over all the earth

When Noah and his family came down from the ark and released all the animals and birds on it to roam across the earth, God said to him:

> The fear of you and the dread of you shall be upon every beast of the earth, and upon every bird of the air, upon everything that creeps on the ground, and all the fish of the sea; into your hand they are delivered. *Genesis 9:2*

In this Noah symbolised the authority to be given to Jesus when, by his delivering work, he too would stand on the earth again with all authority and power over its inhabitants given to him. Jesus said:

> All things have been delivered to me by my father ... all authority in heaven and on earth has been given to me.
> *Matthew 11:27, 28:18*

The same point is made in this passage: "You made him for a little while lower than the angels, you have crowned him with glory and honour, putting everything in subjection under his feet" (Hebrews 2:7-8).

8. A dove symbolised their supreme purpose on earth

When the waters began to recede, Noah sent out a dove three times to see if the land had begun to reappear. The first time it simply returned to him, the second it returned with an olive leaf, and the third it disappeared for good (Genesis 8:8-12). The dove was a symbol that peace had been restored between God and man and the earth.

Likewise, when Jesus was baptised, the Spirit of God descended on him in bodily form, as a dove (Matthew 3:16) and anointed him for his work which he was to accomplish in bringing complete peace and goodwill between God and men (Luke 2:14) with the hope of the redemption of the whole earth (Romans 8:19).

9. Both left a symbol as a legacy of God's saving grace

When the floods had fully receded God promised Noah that never again would the earth be devoured by such a massive flood and he added:

> This is the sign of the covenant which I make between me and you and every living creature that is with you, for all future generations: I set my bow in the cloud, and it shall be a sign of the covenant between me and earth. When I bring clouds over the earth and the bow is seen in the clouds, I will remember my covenant which is between me and every living creature of all flesh; and the waters shall never again become a flood to destroy all flesh.
>
> *Genesis 9:14-15*

Just as the rainbow has become the symbol of God's promise never again to destroy the earth until the final judgment, so Jesus also left a symbol of God's open hand of grace to all men which will never be withdrawn until the end comes:

> The Lord Jesus on the night when he was betrayed took bread, and when he had given thanks, he broke it, and said, "This is my body which is for you. Do this in remembrance of me." In the same way also the cup, after supper, saying, "This cup is the new covenant in my blood. Do this as often as you drink it, in remembrance of me."
>
> *1 Corinthians 11:23-25*

Both Noah and Jesus left a symbol of God's covenant which was put into effect as soon as the storm had passed (in Noah's case, the flood; in Jesus' case, the cross). With Noah it was the rainbow, with Jesus the communion celebration of bread and wine.

10. The days of Jesus and Noah would both be the same

Jesus stated plainly that, when he returns to the earth with the final judgment of God, the earth would be taken by surprise in its daily experiences of life just as it was when the flood came down at the time of Noah:

> As it was in the days of Noah, so it will be in the days of the Son of man. They ate, they drank, they married, they were given in marriage, until the day when Noah entered the ark, and the flood came and destroyed them all ... so it will be on the day when the Son of man is revealed. *Luke 17:26-27,30*

The flood came suddenly, unexpectedly, while all the earth was going about its daily business as if it were just another day. So, Jesus said, it will be when he returns. The heavens will be opened in a moment and the final judgment will come in a moment. Although he said there will be portents hinting its imminent approach, it too will come suddenly while life continues as normal from day-to-day.

The story of Noah, the ark and the flood, has great material for an effective Christian witness to Muslims. During a quiet evening with a Muslim family, why not share the great likenesses between Noah and Jesus and show them how Noah's ark is a symbol of Jesus' saving death and resurrection to newness of life?

Abraham

The Gospel that was Preached to Him

Khalilullah - The Friend of God

I believe the story of Abraham and Isaac is the most powerful and effective source of witness to Muslims from the Old Testament. This is not surprising - Abraham is the great figurehead of all three monotheistic faiths: Judaism, Christianity and Islam. There is so much common ground here and the opportunities for witness abound. We'll look at them in this and the next chapter and shall begin with a description of the patriarch which is common to all three religions - *the friend of God.* In the Jewish Scriptures (a useful description of the Old Testament in discussion with Muslims as opposed to the Christian Scriptures, the New Testament), the designation appears in the following two passages:

> Did you not, O our God, drive out the inhabitants of this land before your people Israel, and give it for ever to the descendants of Abraham your friend? *2 Chronicles 20:7*

> You, Israel, my servant, Jacob whom I have chosen, the offspring of Abraham my friend. *Isaiah 41:8*

Note that in the second passage God himself is recorded as calling Abraham his friend and that the title came not as a result of any writer's impression of the relationship he had with God. When we turn to the Christian Scriptures we find the same title being applied to Abraham in the following text:

> Abraham believed God and it was reckoned to him as righteousness, and he was called the friend of God. *James 2:23*

It may come as a surprise to you to find that the Muslim scripture, the Qur'an, expressly calls Abraham the friend of God as well. Although the title only appears once, like the quotations given from the Bible it is clearly stated and emphasised:

> For Allah did take Ibrahim for a friend. *Surah 4:125*

The word for "a friend" in this verse is khalilaan and, as a result, Abraham is especially known in Islam as *Khalilullah*, the friend of Allah. Moses is called *Kalimatullah*, the word of Allah; David *Khalifatullah*, the representative of Allah; and Jesus *Ruhullah*, the spirit of Allah. Muhammad is known simply as *Rasulullah*, the messenger of Allah. The first question to ask here is obvious - why was Abraham called the Friend of God and what relationship is implied in this title?

Friendships are not based on master-to-servant relationships, nor on the performance of the one party towards the other. Most importantly friendships are built on an acceptance of each other as equals, even though their statuses in life may differ. This verse from the Qur'an helps to illustrate the contrast between friendships and other relationships:

> No one in the heavens and the earth can come to the Compassionate but as a servant. *Surah 19:93*

If so, then the relationship between God and Abraham must have been unique. The title Friend of God implies that there was a deep personal relationship between them and one based on mutual trust and affection. The initiative came from God, indeed it had to for no human being could have approached him as other than a servant, and it is clear that it was God's choice to enter into a relationship with the patriarch on equal terms. Muslims cannot easily explain why Abraham was called God's friend as the Qur'an attempts no explanation of the description, but the Bible does and here the Christian has his first point of witness.

When God first promised Abraham that he would give him a son in his old age, the Bible simply says "he believed the Lord, and he reckoned it to him as righteousness" (Genesis 15:6). This means that Abraham was accepted by God not because of any deeds done in righteousness but because of his complete faith in God. It was simply human faith responding to God's faithfulness. On this basis God took Abraham as his friend. We shall see how this relationship, based on faith alone, leads ultimately to the Gospel of Jesus Christ and how you can witness effectively from it.

The Father of All True Believers

The second point of agreement between Judaism, Christianity and Islam on the person of Abraham is their joint recognition of him as the *father* of all the true people of God. In the Jewish Scriptures we read that God said to Abraham:

> I have made you the father of a multitude of nations.
> *Genesis 17:5*

As a result the Jewish nation claimed to have a special relationship with God and, when Jesus one day accused his Jewish audience of being children of the devil, they boldly declared "Abraham is our father!" (John 8:39). The Christian Scriptures, on the other hand, teach that the true offspring of Abraham are not his physical offspring but those who share the faith of Abraham, the distinct feature that established his unique relationship with God:

> So you see that it is men of faith who are the sons of Abraham ... So then, those who are men of faith are blessed with Abraham who had faith. *Galatians 3:7,9*

Abraham was not approved by God because of any merit he had in himself, not because of his genetic lineage, but because of his faith in God's faithfulness. He is therefore *the father of the faithful*, all true believers who share his faith, not only from the people of Israel but also from the Gentiles, "those who share the faith of Abraham, for he is the father of us all" (Romans 4:16). Interestingly, Abraham is also called the father of those who believe in the Qur'an. These two verses make the point:

> I will make you a leader to the nations. *Surah 2:124*

> Strive hard for Allah with due striving. He has chosen you and has not laid upon you any hardship in your religion, the faith of your father Ibrahim. *Surah 22:78*

The Qur'an follows the New Testament in declaring Abraham to be a leader and example (*imam*) to all mankind (*linnaasi*). Once again he is called the father of all true believers. Here, as in the title Friend of God, Christians have common ground with Muslims and an opportunity to share the Gospel with them. We shall go on to see just how this can be done.

The Promise of a Son to Abraham

Both the Bible and the Qur'an record the express promise of God to Abraham that he would have a son by his wife Sarah. By this time he was nearly a hundred years old and his wife was barren (Romans 4:19). Despite the apparent impossibility that this could happen naturally Abraham trusted God and believed the promise would be fulfilled. It is recorded in the Bible in these words:

> As for Sarai your wife, you shall not call her name Sarai, but Sarah shall be her name. I will bless her, moreover I will give you a son by her; I will bless her, and she shall be a mother of nations; kings of peoples shall come from her ... Sarah your wife will bear you a son, and you shall call his name Isaac. I will establish my covenant with him as an everlasting covenant for his descendants after him.
> *Genesis 17:15-16,19*

The Qur'an confirms the promise and, even though it does not name Abraham's wife, there can be no doubt that it was Sarah. It expressly states that the child of the promise was to be Isaac in these two passages:

> And his wife was standing by, and she laughed; but We gave her glad tidings of Isaac, and after him Jacob.
> *Surah 11:71*

> And We gave him the good news of Isaac, a prophet of the righteous. *Surah 37:112*

Because Abraham trusted in God's faithfulness, he believed the impossible would happen. Note well - it was not because he believed all things were possible to God or that he could simply do anything he wished. He believed, quite simply, that God *would be true to his word.* That is why "no distrust made him waver concerning the promise of God, but he grew strong in his faith as he gave glory to God, fully convinced that God was able to do what he had promised" (Romans 4:20). In witnessing to Muslims it is important to emphasise that it was his faith in God's faithfulness that made him believe God would be faithful to his word and so his son Isaac would be born.

The Command to Sacrifice His Son

In the next chapter we will look at the question of whether it was Isaac or Ishmael whom God called Abraham to sacrifice. Muslims believe it was Ishmael but, as we shall see, the Qur'an does not identify the victim. At this point it is sufficient to deal solely with the subject of the intended sacrifice and you should do the same with Muslims.

When Abraham's son was still a young boy, too young to marry and have any children of his own, the command came to Abraham to sacrifice him. It is recorded in the Bible in these words:

> Take your son, your only son Isaac, whom you love, and go to the land of Moriah, and offer him there as a burnt offering.
>
> *Genesis 22:2*

Muslims credit Abraham for simply being willing to submit to God's command, but here you must go further with them and challenge them to consider what the effect of this sudden demand on him must have been. There are three things the patriarch had to resolve. Muslims acknowledge the first - did he love God enough to be willing to give his son for him? That was the first trial, a test of his love for God, but there were two others where God put himself to the test before Abraham.

Abraham knew God was absolutely holy and trustworthy. In this knowledge he had to resolve how God could command him to do something that was apparently morally questionable and, secondly, he had to ask how God could fulfil his promise to give him a son and, through him, descendants so many that they could not be numbered for multitude (Genesis 16:10) if his son was to be sacrificed before he could even bear a child of his own. It is important to deal with these two questions as they are crucial to the purpose of the sacrifice and its foreshadowing of the sacrifice of God's Son for the sins of the world in a time to come.

During his lifetime Abraham must have witnessed with moral abhorrence and repugnance the idol-worship of his contemporaries. One of the worst practices of idolatry was the sacrifice many idolaters made of their sons to their gods. In a later age Moses himself warned the people of Israel not to enquire how the other nations served their idols that they might imitate them:

> You shall not do so to the Lord your God; for every abominable thing which the Lord hates they have done for their gods; for they even burn their sons and their daughters in the fire to their gods.
>
> *Deuteronomy 12:31*

This, to Moses, was the most abominable practice. Centuries later the evil king Ahaz, who led the nation of Judah into the worship of Baal, also "burned his sons as an offering, according to the abominable practices of the nations whom the Lord drove out before the people of Israel" (2 Chronicles 28:3). How then, Abraham must have asked, could God now command him to offer his son as a *burnt* offering as well? Was he no better than these detestable idols?

In my experience Muslims have no answer to the second test. How could God fulfil his promise that nations would come through Isaac if he was to be sacrificed while still a youngster? The Bible shows that Abraham considered this matter very carefully and, in doing so, came to an astonishing discovery of what God was going to do for the whole human race. It also resolved the first problem, the moral issue. Trusting in God's unflinching faithfulness, Abraham began by presuming that "Every word of God proves true" (Proverbs 30:5). What appeared to be morally reprehensible and physically impossible must in some way be morally excellent and perfectly capable of being fulfilled. Armed with this awareness, based on God's faithfulness, he set out to find out the meaning and purpose of the command to sacrifice his son.

The command to sacrifice seemed to have cut through the promise of a multitude of descendants like a sharp knife cutting a piece of string. As he contemplated first sacrificing his son and then cremating him as a burnt offering, Abraham might have imagined a gust of wind coming down and blowing the ashes away, concluding "there goes the promise of God to the wind." There were four possibilities and I've often canvassed them with Muslims with interesting results. They were:

1. God has forgotten his promise

Fourteen years, the probable age of Abraham's son when the command came to sacrifice him, is a long time. Perhaps God has forgotten his promise? Muslims always react negatively to this suggestion. "God knows everything and never forgets anything." So much for that one.

2. God has changed his mind

Perhaps Isaac has not turned out as well as God might have wished, Abraham might have reasoned. Maybe God has had second thoughts. This one, too, gets short change from Muslims. "God knows all things in advance. He never has to change his mind about anything." This one also soon goes overboard.

3. I'll just submit even though it makes no sense

This is blind faith. Abraham could have simply concluded that he could not resolve the paradox and did not have to. Now God was calling for a sacrifice and he would simply submit to his will. How the promise would be fulfilled, of if it could be, would not be his concern. Here it's not so easy for the Muslim. As we will see in the next chapter, this is exactly what Islam teaches about the *millata-Ibrahim*, the faith of Abraham (Surah 3:95). It sees his faith as an unquestioning submission to God's will and, if Abraham was a prophet of Islam, he might well have chosen this course.

4. God will fulfil his promise!

This is where the Bible's concept of Abraham's faith comes in. Being a faithful God he would not fail to fulfil his word. The question was only, how? When God, at another time, announced to Abraham that he intended to destroy the cities of Sodom and Gomorrah, Abraham argued with him *because he believed God was going against his own faithfulness.* Would God destroy the righteous with the wicked? What if there were fifty righteous people in the cities - would he destroy them with the rest? Abraham cried out to God:

> Far be it from you to do such a thing, to slay the righteous with the wicked, so that the righteous fare as the wicked! Far be that from you! Shall not the Judge of all the earth do right?
>
> *Genesis 18:25*

On the same terms Abraham wrestled with the command to sacrifice his own son. He gave it serious thought. Just as he had previously *considered* the barrenness of Sarah's womb and had *considered* his own body which was as good as dead at a hundred years old when the promise first came (Romans 4:19), so now he did the same. Here is the answer he came up with through the same application of faith in God's faithfulness:

> By faith Abraham, when he was tested, offered up Isaac, and he who had received the promises was ready to offer up his only son, of whom it was said "Through Isaac shall your descendants be named." He considered that God was able to raise men even from the dead, hence, figuratively speaking, he did receive him back.
>
> *Hebrews 11:17-18*

The only way God's promise could be fulfilled was for Isaac to be brought back from the dead after he had been sacrificed. Abraham *considered* this, not because he believed God could perform any miracle, but because it was the only way God could be true to his promise. Let's see what this conclusion led to and how you have here probably the greatest source material to witness to Muslims of the Gospel of Jesus Christ.

Isaac: A Type of the Son of God, Our Saviour

The sun generates light, loads of it. It needs no other object in the sky to assist it to do so. At full moon our satellite reflects the sun's light beautifully, but only marginally. Take away the sun and the moon cannot shine, but remove the moon and the sun will blaze with light undaunted. The moon simply reflects the sun's light as Abraham's faith was a reflection of God's faithfulness. From this principle, and the conclusion that Isaac would rise from the dead, Abraham, the friend of God and father of all true believers, worked it all out.

God is the ultimate Father. Abraham's fatherhood, too, could only be a reflection of it. So, logically, the promised son must also be a reflection, and the sacrifice, and his resurrection from the dead. Abraham foresaw that God would send his own Son into the world, also to be born uniquely, that he would become a sacrifice and, in rising from the dead, would bring a multitude of believers to eternal glory. He worked out the whole Christian Gospel! The New Testament confirms this:

> And the scripture, foreseeing that God would justify the Gentiles by faith, preached the Gospel beforehand to Abraham, saying, "In you shall all the nations be blessed". *Galatians 3:8*

Here Abraham not only worked out how God's promise would still be fulfilled, but saw the glory of it as well. The moral issue was immediately solved. The sacrifice would not imitate pagan degradation, it would be a sign of his love for God which would reflect God's love for us in sending his own son as the saviour of the world. In the end Isaac was spared and Abraham got him back, but God's son would not be spared. Is this all just speculation or coincidence? No, you can show Muslims very easily that it is exactly what happened. When Abraham and Isaac were going up to the chosen place of sacrifice, Isaac said to him "Behold the fire and the wood; but where is the lamb for a burnt offering?" (Genesis 22:7). Abraham's answer is pregnant with foresight:

> God will provide himself the lamb for a burnt offering, my son.
> *Genesis 22:8*

The original Hebrew is more emphatic, it says in effect "God will provide the lamb *from his very own being*." What Abraham was actually saying was "My son, you are to be the sacrifice, but take heart, you are only a reflection of the lamb which God will provide *from himself* as the true sacrifice." Burnt offerings were sin offerings, and Abraham saw that God's own Son would die for the sins of the world. This is confirmed in the following verse where John the Baptist, seeing Jesus pass by, proclaimed:

> Behold, the Lamb of God, who takes away the sin of the world.
> *John 1:29*

There goes the lamb from God whom Abraham foretold! One other verse, where Jesus himself is the speaker, completes the picture. He declared to his Jewish audience:

> Your father Abraham rejoiced that he was to see my day; he saw it and was glad. *John 8:56*

It is in the reassuring words of Genesis 22:8 alone, where Abraham spoke of the lamb of God yet to come, that we can see how he foresaw the day of Jesus to come and rejoiced in it. You can mention that, as Isaac was only a type of Christ and a sinner to be saved like any other human being, he could not fully represent the coming saviour. Only the ram caught in the thicket, a substitution for Isaac, could foreshadow the Son of God who would be substituted for us in enduring the wrath of God against us for all our sins. All this came from nothing more than the nature of Abraham's faith - a response to God's own faithfulness. Seeing his own faith only as a reflection of this, as the moon can only reflects the sun's light, he foresaw the whole Christian Gospel.

I do not know of a more effective way of using the Old Testament prophetic narratives to witness to Muslims of the reality of God's saving grace in Jesus Christ. Once a year, at the end of the Hajj pilgrimage in the middle of the last month of the Muslim year, the whole Islamic world celebrates *Eid ul-Adha*, the Festival of Sacrifice, in commemoration of Abraham's willingness to sacrifice his son in response to God's command. It is the greatest festival of the Muslim year, even outdoing the other great festival at the end of the Ramadan fast, *Eid ul-Fitr*.

So often I have concluded by saying to Muslims "Once a year you observe a man's love for God by being willing to sacrifice his son for him. Every day of the year we commemorate God's love for us by giving his Son as a sacrifice for our sins so that we may be totally forgiven of them and be assured of a place in his kingdom to be revealed on the Last Day." The contrast is devastating. There are very few Muslims who will fail to get the point.

Isaac

The Reflection of the Father's Love

God so Loved the World

Isaac is the perfect type of Christ's first coming to earth. He was born of the Spirit in unique circumstances, thereby prefiguring the virgin-birth; was to be sacrificed as a burnt offering, foreshadowing the redeeming work Jesus was to accomplish at the cross; and was to return to life as a blessing to the nation that would come from him, symbolising the resurrection of Jesus Christ and his saving grace for all who would believe in him. Abraham rightly concluded that it was the *resurrection* that would qualify his son for his unique role and, in this, he foresaw the glory of the risen Saviour, the greater son of Abraham to be revealed at a time yet to come.

In my experience the most effective way of communicating to Muslims exactly what this event means is to focus on the patriarch's uncompromising *love* for God in being willing to sacrifice his son. Muslims always do this. When challenged as to why God would have asked such a sacrifice, they respond by saying it was test of Abraham's love for God. He would prove it was complete if he was willing even to forego his only son. I have often asked Muslims why God did not ask for something less, such as a sacrifice of a hundred sheep, or that he should fast for forty days, or that he should give away half his wealth. They have so often answered me "You do not understand. A son is the dearest thing to a man's heart. If a man will give his son for God, he will give anything for him."

This opens the door to the heart of the Gospel. Abraham was told "Take your son, your *only* son Isaac, whom you *love*" (Genesis 22:2 - emphasis added). God, in calling on Abraham to do this, emphasised the essential nature of the sacrifice. It was, in real terms, a straight choice between his love for God and the object of his deepest affection on earth. Surely if the patriarch would do this, it would prove he would give anything for God. No further proof would be needed. So the Bible says of God's love for us in Christ:

> For God so loved the world that he gave his only Son, that whoever believes in him should not perish but have eternal life.
>
> *John 3:16*

Abraham's love for God in being willing to sacrifice his son for him is the perfect type of God's love for us in giving his Son, Jesus Christ, for the redemption of our souls. Many times I have asked Muslims whether Allah really loves them and, if he does, what he has done to prove it? The answers usually follow the same pattern. They point to the very blessing of their lives, or to times when he has answered their prayers by healing them of diseases or saving them from financial crises. Others have mentioned children they did not think they could have or all their material benefits and possessions. I have always responded by saying that, without doubting that these are all expressions of his kindness and love, that they all cost God nothing and do not affect him at all. What, I have concluded, has God ever done for them that compares with what Abraham was called on to do for him? Has God matched this supreme example of love - a father tearing at the depths of his heart and being willing to give his only son for him? This cost Abraham, indeed it cost him the expression of his very own being - has Allah ever done anything like this in return?

The Muslim can go no further. Allah, in the Qur'an, has done nothing to give something of *himself*, indeed something at the depth of his very own being, to show his absolute love for the human race. The Christian, however, has the perfect answer - Jesus Christ! There was nothing greater that Abraham could sacrifice to prove his surpassing love for God than his son. He was parting with something living that had come from him, something that would cost him far more than all his material possessions put together. Here is the kernel of our witness: God only asked him to do this because *he intended to give his own Son as a sacrifice for our eternal salvation.*

What greater sacrifice could a man make for God than to give his own son for him? What greater proof of God's love can be found than this - that he gave his own Son to die for our sins? And God only required that Abraham should *contemplate* the sacrifice. God, on the other hand, actually *went right through* with his love for men by giving his Son Jesus to die for us so that we might live in him.

> In *this* the love of God was made manifest among us, that God sent his only Son into the world, so that we might live through him.
>
> *1 John 4:9*

Just as Isaac willingly showed complacency with the will of God, so Jesus of his own free will voluntarily laid down his life for us. If God had redeemed us through anything he had created, it would have cost him nothing for he created it out of nothing. But God never asked any man to do more for him that he was willing to do in return. Isaac had come from his father's body. So God gave his own Son for us - one who was not created but whose blessed presence the Father had enjoyed from all eternity. Notice that in this story it is the father's love that it is emphasised in being willing to give his son. Point out to Muslims that it shows that the death of Jesus was not something that happened to him while his Father simply looked on. The Father *gave* his only Son - it was an awesome expression of his own love for us in being willing to sacrifice what was dearest to his own heart.

There can only be a few Muslims who will not be moved by the comparison. Islam, ultimately, leaves them with an imbalance they can hardly explain. A man was commanded to show his love for Allah in a way which Allah has never matched for mankind in return. Can this really be true? Can a man's love for God, fully expressed, surpass God's love for mankind? Christianity has the golden answer! Abraham's love was only a *reflection*, a shadow, of the supreme love God was destined to show us in the gift of his Son. Abraham's love for God could not have been tested more deeply. Could the depth of God's love for mankind have been proved in any way greater than this, that he sent his Son to become our Saviour? Can this be surpassed?

> In *this* is love, not that we loved God, but that he loved us, *and* sent his Son to be the expiation of our sins. *1 John 4:10*

The Eid-ul-Adha festival commemorates an act of love by a man for God which, in its excellence, has no parallel from heaven in return. Allah has given man *things* - children, health, possessions, religion - but he has given him nothing of *himself*. It is like a man who bestows gifts on his beloved but never gives himself to her in marriage. Ask a Muslim this simple question - if the greatest way a man could show his love for God was to be willing to sacrifice his son for him, what is the greatest way God could ever show his love for us? There can only be one answer.

You can go further. God's love for us in Christ far overshadows Abraham's love for him. Abraham, a man of dust, was prepared to give his son, also made of dust, for the God of glory in heaven. An obligation rested on him to be obedient to God's command. But what obligation was laid on the God of glory in heaven to give his Son, who shares his eternal glory to the full, for sinful men of dust on the surface of a minor planet? Again, God spared the son of Abraham. He did not spare his own Son.

> He who did not spare his own Son but gave him for us all, will he not also give us all things with him? *Romans 8:32*

Once a year the Muslim world remembers a man's sacrificial love for God but every day of the year Christians celebrate God's sacrificial love for mankind and honour his wondrous grace in securing our salvation - and that so that we could receive it as a gift! (Romans 6:23). I do not believe there is a greater contact point in the lives of the former prophets and patriarchs where Christians have a more powerful witness resource to Muslims than here.

True Faith - Submission or a Response to God's Faithfulness?

We go back to the subject of Abraham's faith. We saw in the last chapter that it was a response to God's faithfulness. It is important to see how the Qur'an regards Abraham's faith, especially as it uses the same expression found in Romans 4:16 to define it. It appears in this verse:

> Say: Allah has spoken the truth. Follow therefore the faith of Abraham, the upright, who was not one of the idolaters.
> *Surah 3:95*

The expression "the faith of Abraham" reads, in the original Arabic, *millata-Ibrahim*. The word *millah* appears fifteen times in the Qur'an and on seven occasions it is used directly in association with Abraham (cf. Surahs 2:130, 2:135, 6:161). At face value the Qur'an appears to be confirming what the Bible teaches about Abraham, namely that his faith is an example of the faith all believers should have in God (Galatians 3:6-9) but, on closer inspection, we get a very different picture. The following verse defines the relationship between God and Abraham:

> Recall when his Lord said to him: "Submit!," he replied "I submit to the Lord of the worlds". *Surah 2:131*

The command in the Arabic original is simply Aslim - Submit! Abraham's reply is *aslamtu* - I submit. Both words come from the same root letters (*sin, lam, mim*) as the words *Islam* (Submission) and Muslim (one who submits). Abraham is said, in the Qur'an, not to have been a Jew or a Christian but a *haniffaam-muslimaan*, "an upright man and one who submits." Thus he is a prototype of a true Muslim. Abraham's faith, therefore, is defined as no more than an unquestioning obedience and submission to the commands of Allah. His willingness to sacrifice his son is not seen as an act of love towards Allah, contrary to what Muslims freely assert, but solely as a submission to the inevitable. He did not question the command to sacrifice, he simply obeyed it. It appears he did not work it through on the basis that God would be true to his promises, nor did he determine his response as an act of faith in God's faithfulness. He took the third option we mentioned earlier, namely blind faith, a simple acquiesence with the will of God irrespective of the circumstances or implications. In the story of the sacrifice in the Qur'an we get a very clear definition of his response:

> When they had both submitted and he had thrown him down on his forehead, We called out to him: O Abraham! You have already fulfilled the vision. *Surah 37:103-105*

Both Abraham and his son are marked out for their *submission* to Allah's command. The words used in the original Arabic are *falamma aslama* - "they had both submitted," and once again the word for "submitted" comes from the same root letters as Islam and Muslim. While the Qur'an may characterise Abraham's faith consistently with its whole concept of what Islam is, it is a poor shadow and substitute for what that faith really was. The Bible shows that he did not simply respond "I submit" as a dog unthinkingly does when you issue the command "heel!," rather it reveals how the patriarch wrestled with the command which appeared not only to be morally questionable but also seemed to cut right through the promises he had previously received. In the Bible Abraham deals with this by responding to God's *faithfulness*, in the Qur'an he simply responds to his will, and there is a huge difference between the two.

In the Bible Abraham considers what he knows about God, in the Qur'an he reacts to no more than what he hears from God. Unfortunately this comparison defines the whole difference between Islam and Christianity - we know the Lord, we have been saved by his grace, we are his children and we have experienced the greatest act of his love for mankind. Muslims, on the contrary, worship a God they neither know nor can truly love. Here is an open door for a witness to God's glorious grace in his Son Jesus Christ!

Ishaq or Ismail - The Muslim Dilemma

Which son was saved from being sacrificed, Isaac or Ishmael? Muslims universally believe that it was Ishmael and that the event took place near Mina, a village a few miles east of Mecca. Both the Jewish and Christian Scriptures plainly state that it was Isaac (Genesis 22:2, Hebrews 11:17, James 2:21) and it is most significant to find that the Qur'an does not say which son it was. The story of the call to Abraham to sacrifice his son and what followed is recorded in Surah 37:100-113 but the Qur'an does not identify the son. This is strange, and if a Muslim challenges you and claims it was Ishmael, you can ask why the Qur'an is silent on the matter if it came to confirm the former scriptures (Surah 5:48) and was sent to clear up any differences of opinion (Surah 16:64).

The argument that it was Ishmael is based on two premises. Firstly, God called Abraham to sacrifice his only son and, as Ishmael preceded Isaac, it must have been him. Secondly, just after the narrative in the Qur'an the book says:

> And we announced to him Isaac, a prophet of the righteous, and we blessed him and Isaac. *Surah 37:112-113*

It is argued that this statement *follows* the story of the sacrifice and therefore it must have been *another* son of Abraham who submitted to Allah's command, namely Ishmael. We'll give you the key answers to Muslims on the issues here.

1. Sarah and Hagar

No Muslim doubts that Sarah was the mother of Isaac and Hagar the mother of Ishmael. Significantly Sarah is mentioned on a few occasions in the Qur'an but Hagar never. Also, Sarah is expressly said to be *the only wife* of Abraham in the book, as in this verse:

> And his wife was standing by, wondering. Then We announced to her the good news of Isaac, and from the progeny of Isaac, Jacob.
> *Surah 11:71*

In another passage, when Allah confirms the promise of a son to Abraham, "his wife came up" and smote her face, bewailing her barrenness as an old woman (Surah 51:28-29). In both cases the *singular* is used for the word "wife", namely *imra'ah.* Not only is Hagar not mentioned in the Qur'an but the book, by implication, makes it clear she was never the wife of Abraham. A tradition in the Sirat literature confirms that Hagar was only a servant in Abraham's household when Sarah gave her to her husband to bear him a son:

> Then he called Hagar who was the most trustworthy of his servants, and he bestowed her (Hagar) on her (Sarah) and gave her clothes; subsequently Sarah made a gift of her (Hagar) to Ibrahim who cohabited with her and she bore Ismail who was the eldest of his children.
>
> *Ibn Sa'd, Kitab al-Tabaqat al-Kabir, Vol.1, p.41*

Quite clearly Hagar was never the wife of Abraham but only the maid of his wife Sarah. Thus it was quite proper for God to speak of Isaac as Abraham's only son, namely his only *legitimate* son of his wife Sarah. This is strengthened by the fact that Hagar and Ishmael had parted from Abraham many years earlier (Genesis 21:14).

2. "We blessed him and Isaac"

No Muslim can dogmatically say that it was Ishmael who was to be sacrificed in the light of the Qur'an's silence on the subject. There is a double testimony from both the previous scriptures that it was Isaac and, if the Qur'an had come to clarify any previous errors or points of dispute as it claims, it would surely have named Ishmael if he was the chosen victim. Ishmael is specifically named as the helper of Abraham when, as the Qur'an alleges, he built the Ka'aba (Surah 2:127). Significantly early Muslim historians differed on the identity of the son while no such confusion has ever existed between Jews and Christians. Also, Surah 37 mentions many of the prophets by name (Noah, Abraham, Isaac, Moses, Aaron, Elijah, Lot and Jonah) and the omission of Ishmael is remarkable if he was the son to be offered in the only passage in the Qur'an where the event is recorded.

There is a clear symmetry between these clauses: "when they had both submitted, (Surah 37:103) and "We blessed him and Isaac" (Surah 37:113). As Abraham and Isaac had both fully submitted themselves to the will of Allah that the one should sacrifice the other, it was only reasonable that his blessings should come on both of them. Furthermore the Qur'an confirms that the child to be sacrificed was originally promised to Abraham: "We announced to him an upright boy" (Surah 37:101). The Qur'an on a number of occasions confirms that Isaac was specifically promised to Abraham but nowhere says anything similar about Ishmael. If we are to believe the Qur'an when it claims to clarify everything that preceded it in the former scriptures, we must presume the son to be sacrificed was Isaac.

3. The Scripture and the Prophethood

You can emphasise the special role of Isaac as the promised son by pointing out to Muslims that God's covenant was made through his line and not Ishmael's. This is clearly stated in the Bible:

> And Abraham said to God, "O that Ishmael might live in thy sight!" God said, "No, but Sarah your wife shall bear you a son, and you shall call his name Isaac. I will establish my covenant with him as an everlasting covenant for his descendants after him. As for Ishmael, I have heard you; behold, I will bless him and make him fruitful and multiply him exceedingly; he shall be the father of twelve princes, and I will make him a great nation. *But I will establish my covenant with Isaac*, whom Sarah shall bear to you at this season next year". *Genesis 17:18-21*

There is another passage in the Qur'an which testifies to the preference of Allah for Isaac and his offspring as the medium of his coming salvation rather than the line of Ishmael. It is significant to find, once again, that the Qur'an takes no issue with the Bible but confirms that God's covenant was to come through Isaac:

> And we granted him Isaac and Jacob and ordained through his progeny the Prophethood and the Scripture.
> *Surah 29:27*

This is an emphatic statement. The *Nubuwwah* (prophetic line) and *Kitaab* (scripture) were to come through his offspring alone. The Bible confirms this in Romans 9:4-5. So the Qur'an confirms the covenant and the superiority of Isaac over Ishmael, hence it must be concluded that as the intended sacrificial victim was announced to Abraham beforehand, it could only have been Isaac and not Ishmael.

In conclusion it is useful to point out to Muslims that as it was Isaac and not Ishmael who was expressly promised, that the covenant of God was made through his line including the Prophethood and Scripture, and that he was born in a unique manner as opposed to Ishmael who was born by a simple illegitimate union, Isaac is obviously the more prominent of the two men. Once it is accepted that he was the son to be sacrificed, the whole purpose of his life comes into focus. He was a type and a symbol of the Messiah to come after the line of Prophethood and the prophecies of the Scriptures would have their fulfilment. You can freely challenge Muslims to become followers of the ultimate Son of Abraham, Jesus Christ, whom God has set forth as the one and only true Saviour of the whole human race, and whom Isaac prefigured. The Apostle Paul brings out the ultimate distinction between Isaac and Ishmael very concisely in these words:

> Now we, brethren, like Isaac, are children of promise ... we are not children of the slave but of the free woman.
>
> *Galatians 4:28,31*

Why does the Qur'an not name the son to be offered as a sacrifice and, immediately thereafter, name Isaac twice as the promised son of Abraham? Perhaps Muhammad was uncertain about the identity of the son and, though he might have wished it was Ishmael, he might have been aware that he is an insignificant and irrelevant figure in the Bible in comparison with Isaac. Hence he left the identity an open question. If, however, Isaac is overlooked as the intended victim, the whole character of the event as a type and symbol of God's coming salvation in his Son Jesus is missed completely and, with it for the Muslim world, the hope of eternal life.

Joseph

A Symbol of the Coming Deliverer

Sons Who Became Servants

The story of Joseph in the Qur'an is rather unique in that a whole chapter is given to it, Surah 12 which is appropriately titled *Suratu-Yusuf*, yet no mention of the patriarch appears anywhere else in the book. The Qur'an actually states that, until the story came to him in one complete narrative, Muhammad had "been among those who knew it not" (Surah 12:3). Significantly the Qur'an suggests, in the same verse, that he only heard of it because it was revealed to him by Allah. Non-Muslims will conclude that he was simply ignorant of it until he heard it retold somewhere in all its details which, like most Qur'anic stories of the prophets, are partly Biblical and partly traditional. Nonetheless its inclusion in the book creates further opportunities to show how the life and work of Jesus was foreshadowed in the lives of many of the prophets who went before him. One simple definition of the story in the same text we have referred to, however, is a tremendous platform for a witness of God's saving grace in Jesus Christ. It is:

> We do relate to you the most beautiful of stories.
>
> *Surah 12:3*

If the story of Joseph is beautiful, how much more is the story of Jesus which it prefigures! A brief outline of their lives and achievements from the Bible can be put together to show just how similar their courses were. Joseph's whole life is defined in this brief passage:

> When he summoned a famine on the land, and broke every staff of bread, he had sent a man ahead of them, Joseph, who was sold as a slave. His feet were hurt with fetters, his neck was put in a collar of iron; until what he said came to pass the word of the Lord tested him. The king sent and released him, the rulers of the people set

> him free; he made him lord of his house, and ruler of all his possessions, to instruct his princes at his pleasure, and to teach his elders wisdom. *Psalm 105:16-22*

The parallel passage to this one in the Bible, which defines the life, work and ultimate achievements of Jesus Christ, is this one:

> Have this mind among yourselves, which is yours in Christ Jesus, who, though he was in the form of God, did not count equality with God a thing to be grasped, but emptied himself, taking the form of a servant, being born in the likeness of men. And being found in human form he humbled himself and became obedient to death, even death on a cross. Therefore God has highly exalted him and bestowed on him the name which is above every name, that at the name of Jesus every knee should bow, in heaven and on earth and under the earth, and every tongue confess that Jesus Christ is Lord, to the glory of God the Father. *Philippians 2:5-11*

The first thing to note is that both of them, after being honoured as sons in their father's houses, became servants in another realm. Joseph "was sold as a slave" and Jesus "took the form of a servant, being born in the likeness of men." Before this Joseph had been the beloved son of Jacob more than any of his other children (Genesis 37:3) and he made a coat of many colours to adorn him. Jesus likewise, when praying to his Father in heaven, spoke of the "glory which I had with you before the world was made" (John 17:5). From here on Joseph becomes a type of Christ, probably the most perfect type in the whole of the Old Testament. Of all the great figureheads in the Old Testament, Joseph's life is the only one without blemish. No major downfall or scandal is reported of him like Moses' murder of an Egyptian, Noah's drunkenness, David's adultery or Solomon's profligacy. The Qur'an goes on to say:

> Truly in Joseph and his brethren there are signs for seekers.
> *Surah 12:7*

Indeed! Here you, in witnessing to Muslims, can show them just what those signs are. We will look at some of the remarkable parallels between Joseph and Jesus and see how the Gospel was prefigured in Joseph's life.

Comparisons between the sufferings of Joseph and Jesus

Once Joseph had been sold to the Ishmaelites by his brothers, he was taken down to Egypt. There he was sold to Potiphar, an officer of Pharaoh and the captain of his guard. Although this turned to his advantage for a while because of his great service and faithfulness to his master, one event soured his life yet again. Potiphar so trusted him that he had "made him overseer of his house and put him in charge of all that he had" (Genesis 39:4) but his wife "cast her eyes upon Joseph" (v.7) and tried to persuade him to lie with her. She did this for many days until one day, when she caught him by his garment, he fled, leaving it in her hands (v.12). It's well known what happened next and from here on let's look at the similarities between Jesus and Joseph.

1. They were both severely tempted to sin against God

Joseph said to Potiphar's wife, "How then can I do this great wickedness, and sin against God?" (Genesis 39:9). Jesus likewise, when he was in the wilderness, was forcefully tempted by Satan on three occasions to break faith with his Father. He said to the devil:

> It is written, "You shall worship the Lord your God, and him only shall you serve". *Luke 4:7*

2. Both Joseph and Jesus were falsely accused

Although Joseph refused to listen to Potiphar's wife, even though she tempted him for many days, she falsely accused him to her husband in these words:

> The Hebrew servant, whom you have brought among us, came in to me to insult me; but as soon as I lifted up my voice and cried, he left his garment with me, and fled out of the house.
> *Genesis 39:17-18*

As a result of this false charge Joseph was thrown into prison (v.20). Jesus was also falsely accused by the chief priests before Pontius Pilate in these words:

> We found this man perverting our nation, and forbidding us to give tribute to Caesar, and saying that he himself is Christ a king.
> *Luke 23:2*

This charge, too, was patently false as, when Jesus was asked by the Pharisees and Herodians whether it was lawful to pay taxes to Caesar, he replied "Render therefore to Caesar the things that are Caesar's, and to God the things that are God's" (Matthew 22:21). In another passage we read that "many false witnesses came forward" to give false testimony against Jesus at his trial (Matthew 26:60).

3. They were both rejected by their own people

When Joseph went to look for his brethren and found them at Dothan, they conspired against him, stripped him of his robe, and cast him into a pit (Genesis 37:23-24). After first agreeing to kill him, they changed their minds and decided to sell him as a slave to the Ishmaelites. Stephen, in his address to the chief priests, described the outcome in these words:

> And the patriarchs, jealous of Joseph, sold him into Egypt; but God was with him, and rescued him out of all his afflictions, and gave him favour and wisdom before Pharaoh, king of Egypt, who made him governor over Egypt and over all his household.
>
> *Acts 7:9-10*

Jesus, too, was rejected by the Israelites. "He came to his own home, and his own people received him not" (John 1:11). On one occasion they tried to throw him down headlong from the brow of the hill on which their city Nazareth was built (Luke 4:29), on another they sought to stone him to death (John 10:31). Like Joseph, Jesus was delivered up because of the envy of his own people which Pilate clearly perceived (Mark 15:10)

4. They were both sold for a price

The brothers of Joseph profited from his betrayal (Genesis 37:27). The Qur'an has an interesting comment at this point:

> They sold him for a miserable price, a few dirhams numbered, and they were indifferent to him. *Surah 12:20*

Jesus, too, was sold and betrayed for "a miserable price." When Judas went to the chief priests and offered to deliver him into their hands, they paid him thirty pieces of silver (Matthew 26:14).

5. Both of them won the approval of their captors

After Joseph had been thrown into prison the Lord "gave him favour in the sight of the keeper of the prison" (Genesis 39:21) who committed all the prisoners to his care and, convinced of his integrity, did not expect him to account to him (v.23).

Likewise the Roman centurion, who was keeping guard over Jesus and the two thieves who were crucified with him, was also persuaded of his integrity and, as Jesus breathed his last, he cried out "Certainly this man was innocent!" (Luke 23:47).

6. They both predicted the destiny of their fellow-prisoners

Just as Joseph had been thrown into prison as a criminal with the other prisoners present, so Jesus too had been condemned to die with two other prisoners and had been crucified with them. Here comes one of the most interesting and significant parallels between them. Two of the prisoners interned with Joseph were the Pharaoh's chief butler and chief baker. One night they both had strange dreams and Joseph encouraged them to reveal them to him (Genesis 40:8).

The chief butler told Joseph that he had seen a vine and, when its branches budded and blossomed, he took the grapes, pressed them into Pharaoh's cup, and placed the cup in Pharaoh's hand (Genesis 40:10-12). Joseph assured him that he would be saved and delivered out of the prison within three days, adding that he would also be restored to his position as Pharaoh's butler. When the chief baker saw the interpretation was favourable, he too told Joseph his dream. There were three cake baskets on his head with all sorts of baked food for Pharaoh, but the birds were plundering it. Joseph told him he would be condemned, that Pharaoh would hang him on a tree, and that the birds would eat his flesh (Genesis 40:19). The outcome is expressed in the Qur'an in these words:

> O my two fellow-prisoners! As to one of you, he will pour out wine for his lord to drink; as for the other, he will be crucified, so that the birds will eat from his head. *Surah 12:41*

Jesus was crucified between two thieves who had been condemned with him. Like the jailer and butler, he promised salvation to the one and left the other to go to perdition. Jesus said to the first:

> Truly, I say to you, today you will be with me in Paradise.
> *Luke 23:43*

This is a remarkable parallel between the two stories and here we see Joseph foreshadowing the role of Jesus who is the source of salvation to all who believe in him but who will be the judge of all who don't.

7. Both asked those around them to remember them

This may be no more than a coincidence (the last illustration is definitely not!) but both Joseph and Jesus asked to be remembered. Joseph said to the chief butler:

> But remember me, when it is well with you, and do me the kindness, I pray you, to make mention of me to Pharaoh, and so get me out of this house. *Genesis 40:14*

Joseph's request to the butler to mention him to Pharaoh is repeated in the Qur'an in Surah 12:42. Jesus also asked his disciples to bring his redeeming death to mind whenever they met together to eat bread and drink wine:

> Do this in remembrance of me. *Luke 22:19*

8. Joseph and Jesus both forgave their enemies

Many years after Joseph had been released from prison and had become the most important leader in Egypt under Pharaoh, his brothers came to the land because the famine was severe in Canaan and they had heard there was grain in Egypt. After they had recognised the lord of the granaries to be Joseph their brother, they feared he would avenge himself on them for selling him into slavery but he replied:

> Fear not, for am I in the place of God? As for you, you meant evil against me; but God meant it for good, to bring it about that many people should be kept alive, as they are today. So do not fear; I will provide for you and your little ones. *Genesis 50:19-21*

When Jesus was crucified, instead of anticipating his resurrection when he could wreak vengeance on those who had condemned him, he prayed as follows:

> Father, forgive them, for they know not what they do.
> *Luke 23:34*

Their Eventual Glory and Honour

Joseph's ability to interpret dreams by the power of God eventually turned his life around. When Pharaoh had two similar dreams and no one could interpret them, the chief butler remembered Joseph and he was called before

Pharaoh. He told him his two dreams were one. The fat stalks and cows represented seven years of plenty. The thin stalks and cows, which consumed them but remained gaunt, represented seven years of famine. Joseph advised Pharaoh to store up grain during the good years so that there would be plenty when the famine came. Pharaoh's response to Joseph was:

> Since God has shown you all this, there is none so discreet and wise as you are; you shall be over my house, and all my people shall order themselves as you command; only as regards the throne will I be greater than you. *Genesis 41:39-40*

This is a picture of all authority in heaven and on earth being given to Jesus after his resurrection and ascension to heaven with all things subject to him. As with Joseph, the only exception would be that he would remain subject to his Father. This passage brings out the parallel perfectly:

> But when it says, "All things are put in subjection under him," it is plain that he is excepted who put all things under him. When all things are subjected to him, then the Son himself will be subjected to him who put all things under him, that God may be everything to every one. *1 Corinthians 15:27-28*

Joseph, who had previously been condemned, was now invested with great honour over all the land of Egypt and he became its saviour, making grain available not only to the Egyptians but to the nations round about, to keep them alive until the famine had passed. So Jesus, who had also been condemned, rose to heaven where he was to receive "power and wealth and wisdom and might and honour and glory and blessing" (Revelation 5:12).

Two points in the Qur'an are also worth noting at this point. Pharaoh is recorded as saying of Joseph: "Bring him to me, I will keep him about myself" (Surah 12:54), a statement reflecting the glory of Jesus who now reigns at the right hand of the Father where he will be for evermore (Acts 7:56). Joseph, also, is recorded as saying to Pharaoh "Set me over the store-houses of the land, I am a good keeper, knowledgeable" (Surah 12:55). This too parallels the following statement about Jesus in the Bible: "Christ was faithful over God's house as a son" (Hebrews 3:6).

Joseph typifies the life of Jesus in every aspect and here the Christian has a great foundation for witnessing to Muslims. A very interesting summary concludes the Qur'an's record of the life of Joseph as recorded in its twelfth chapter:

> In their histories there is indeed a lesson for men of understanding. It is not a narrative which could be forged, but a verification of what is before it, and a distinct explanation of all things, and a guide and a mercy to a people who believe. *Surah 12:111*

You too can be a guide, and show the mercy of Jesus to Muslims, by comparing the lives of Joseph and Jesus and showing how the great patriarch foreshadowed the life, suffering and subsequent glory of the Christian Saviour.

Moses

Law and Grace in Sharp Contrast

The Old and New Covenants

Muslims often ask why Christians have an Old and New Testament in their Bible. What was wrong with the Old Testament that you had to have a New? Isn't the new a corrupted version of the Old which was the original scripture? Why do you have to have two testaments at all? When these questions are asked Christians have a wonderful opportunity to witness to Muslims of God's saving grace in Jesus Christ.

There is a simple answer to these questions, of course. The Qur'an talks about two books in the possession of the Jews and Christians, namely *at-Tawraat* (the Law) and *al-Injil* (the Gospel) respectively (Surah 5:69, 7:157). The former is said to have been delivered to Moses, the latter to Jesus. Christians need only explain that there were two different scriptures, as the Qur'an testifies, which date from the time of two different religious leaders, Moses and Jesus.

Yet the essential distinction between the two books is the foundation for a very positive witness, namely the old and new covenants. The first covenant, given to Moses, was one based on a series of laws, rituals and regulations. It placed the responsibility for observing these rules squarely on the shoulders of the Israelites who received them. These quotes help to make the point:

> You shall not kill. You shall not commit adultery. You shall not steal. You shall not bear false witness against your neighbour.
>
> *Exodus 20:13-16*

> You shall not hate your brother in your heart, but you shall reason with your neighbour, lest you bear sin because of him. You shall not take vengeance or bear any grudge against the sons of your own

> people, but you shall love your neighbour as yourself. You shall keep my statutes. *Leviticus 19:17-19*

Throughout the books of Moses, where the original terms of the old covenant are set out, the commands are the same. "You shall, you shall not" introduces each one. It was up to the Israelites exclusively to keep these laws, either by fulfilling the acts of obedience that were commanded, or by refraining from actions that were prohibited. The important issue here is the response of the whole nation to these laws. When Moses went up Mount Sinai to receive the two tablets of the law (Exodus 24:12) and stayed there many days, the Israelites rebelled and ordered Aaron to create golden images as gods to go before them rather than the Lord. They made a golden calf and worshipped and sacrificed to it (Exodus 32:8). They indulged themselves in what we today would call an orgy (Exodus 32:6).

In one fell swoop they broke virtually every one of the ten commandments they had received, especially the cardinal laws commanding them to worship God alone and not to make graven images and go after them. This expression of hostility to God's laws characterised their relationship with him throughout the exodus and symbolises the inner animosity in the heart of every man towards God's holy statutes (Jeremiah 17:9). As a result of their rebellion 3000 men of Israel who had spearheaded the rebellion were put to the sword and destroyed for their transgression.

God's patience with Israel was sustained for many centuries to come but by the time of Jeremiah he concluded that they would never bow to his holy laws and would always disobey him. He told them their hurt was incurable and that there was no one who would uphold their cause (Jeremiah 30:12). He had dealt them the blow of a enemy because their guilt was great (v.14). He warned them that Jerusalem would become a heap of ruins (Jeremiah 26:18), yet in his love for them he promised he would not make a full end of them (Jeremiah 30:11). While he was satisfied that they had forsaken his covenant to the point where it had finally been abrogated, yet he would press on with them. He gave his reason in this famous passage:

> I have loved you with an everlasting love; therefore I have continued my faithfulness to you. Again I will build you, and you shall be built, O virgin Israel! *Jeremiah 31:3-4*

Only a few verses later in the same chapter we read God's promise that he would make a new covenant with them unlike the covenant he had made with their forefathers through Moses. This was the covenant he would make:

> I will put my law within them, and I will write it upon their hearts; and I will be their God, and they shall be my people ... I will forgive their iniquity, and I will remember their sin no more.
>
> *Jeremiah 31:33-34*

Note the shift in emphasis. The new covenant was not based on a "You shall, you shall not" foundation but rather on God's promise "I will put, I will write, I will forgive." God was electing to take the responsibility for the successful outworking of the relationship between him and them on himself! He was binding himself to them in an eternal covenant, holding himself responsible for their faithfulness. By no longer writing his laws on tablets of stone but rather on human hearts, written not with ink but with the Spirit of the living God (2 Corinthians 3:3), he would assure their obedience. Much the same theme is found in this passage where the promised new covenant is again canvassed:

> I will sprinkle clean water upon you, and you shall be clean from all your uncleannesses and from all your idols I will cleanse you. A new heart I will give you, and a new spirit I will put within you.
>
> *Ezekiel 37:25-26*

Here is a glorious opportunity to witness to Muslims of the real reason why Jesus Christ came to earth. He came to fulfil the new covenant which, he said, would be done through the giving of his shed blood for the forgiveness of our sins (1 Corinthians 11:25). Through his death and resurrection our sins were paid for and the doors of heaven were opened for the very Spirit of God himself to enter into the heart of every true believer and unite him to God. It is not coincidental that when the Holy Spirit was poured out on the Day of Pentecost, 3000 of those who heard the word believed and were baptised (Acts 2:41). It was exactly the same number of those who had defied the Lord when the first covenant was introduced, and who perished for their rebellion. The law given through Moses brought death to 3000, the grace of God brought the Spirit and eternal life to the same number who heard's Peter's message of salvation in Jesus Christ. You have much material for witness here through the God "who has made us competent to be ministers of a new covenant, not in a written code, but in the Spirit, for the written code kills, but the Spirit gives life" (2 Corinthians 2:6).

Jesus Christ Mediates a Greater Covenant

From other passages of scripture, especially the Book of Hebrews, you can strengthen the case for the new covenant, especially the fact that it is a far superior one to the old, not least because the one who mediates it is far superior to Moses. The difference is defined in this text:

> Jesus has been counted worthy of as much more glory than Moses as the builder of a house has more honour than the house.
>
> *Hebrews 3:3*

The passage goes on to explain the difference - Moses was faithful in all God's house as a *servant* but Christ was faithful over God's house as a *Son* (Hebrews 3:5-6). Moses was no more than the spokesman for God's first covenant and could not cleanse the Israelites of their transgressions against it. But Jesus, through his death and resurrection, opened the way for men to be directly forgiven by God and, being both God and man, was able to reconcile man to God and unite true believers through the Holy Spirit who was now free to enter their hearts. The effect of this is summed up in these words:

> But as it is, Christ has obtained a ministry which is as much more excellent than the old as the covenant he mediates is better, since it is enacted on better promises. *Hebrews 8:6*

The important thing is to show that we, as Christians, have a far greater hope in this awesome covenant which is far superior to the old, especially as Muslims are taught that all the prophets were the same and that Jesus and Muhammad merely confirmed the first covenant of the law which God gave to Moses. It is useful always to bear in mind that Islam views the whole religious course of history as a level playing field. The religion of Moses is said to be identical to the religion of Muhammad - a set of moral laws, ceremonial rituals and other observances. Yet our faith is based on a rising crescendo to a climax: God's glorious revelation of himself in Jesus, his salvation through the cross, and our potential to live for ever and become the sons and daughters of God through his resurrection to life. It is also important to emphasise the futility of the partial observance of God's laws when our sins separate us inevitably from God. All the rites and sacrifices in the world cannot remedy this malady.

> According to this arrangement, gifts and sacrifices are offered which cannot perfect the conscience of the worshipper, but deal only with food and drink and various ablutions, regulations for the body imposed until the time for reformation.
>
> *Hebrews 9:9-10*

This is the shortcoming of Islam also. It is filled with specific laws about fasting, the times and direction of the five daily prayers, the observance of the Hajj pilgrimage, the acceptability (*halaal*) or otherwise (*haraam*) of various foods, and the like. All these cannot redeem the seared consciences and paralysed souls of men and women who have sinned against God and live in complete separation from him. Only Jesus can do this. Only he can secure our forgiveness and impart the Spirit of God to us so that we become alive to God again in our hearts and live in eternal communion with him.

Moses and Jesus in John's Gospel

There is another source for showing the superiority of Jesus over Moses and it is the Gospel of John. Here deliberate comparisons are drawn between them to bring out not only the greater glory of Jesus the mediator of God's greater covenant, but also the difference between the law and grace as seen in the ministries of these two men. John introduces this subject with these words:

> For the law was given through Moses, grace and truth came through Jesus Christ. *John 1:17*

1. The Brass Serpent

Proving the superiority of Jesus over the former patriarchs is a favourite theme in John's Gospel. He demonstrates the superiority of Jesus over Abraham (John 8:58), over Jacob (John 4:12-14) and over John the Baptist (John 3:28-29), but most of his attention, understandably, is given to the greatest of all the Old Testament figureheads, Moses, the mediator of the first covenant. The first example appears in this text where Jesus Christ is the speaker:

> And as Moses lifted up the serpent in the wilderness, so must the Son of man be lifted up, that whoever believes in him may have eternal life. *John 3:14-15*

Jesus is referring to an incident recorded in the book of Numbers. As the people of Israel retraced their passage through the Sinai wilderness and had to go back towards the Red Sea to get around the land of Edom, they became impatient and accused Moses of bringing them out only to die in the desert for lack of water and food. Once again God's anger was kindled against them:

> Then the Lord sent fiery serpents among the people, and they bit the people, so that many of the people of Israel died.
>
> *Numbers 21:6*

In anguish the people confessed their rebellion to Moses and acknowledged their guilt, pleading with Moses to beseech the Lord to remove the serpents from among them. God, however, ordered Moses to make a brass serpent and to nail it to a pole in the midst of the camp so that, whenever anyone was bitten, they could look at the brass serpent and be healed.

The comparison Jesus draws between his own destiny and the serpent is a useful basis for witness by itself. Jesus too would be lifted up, publicly portrayed as crucified, and salvation is found for all who turn and believe in him. Just as the brass serpent was made in the image of the fiery serpents biting the Israelites, but did not possess the deadly venom that was killing them, so Jesus became sin for us (2 Corinthians 5:21), the deadly affliction that destroys all men, but did not have any sin of his own (2 Peter 2:22). There is a beautiful stained glass window at the west end of Norwich Cathedral in England which contains a portrayal of the brass serpent to which Moses points for the renewal of the stricken Israelites below a representation of the crucifixion of Jesus for the salvation of all mankind.

The important point here, however, is the superiority of Jesus over Moses. The brass serpent served for the temporary healing of the Israelites struck down by the venom of the fiery serpents, but Jesus was to be lifted up so that all who believe in him might have *eternal* life. The miracle done through Moses did not stop the stricken Israelites from dying another day in the wilderness, yet the death and miraculous resurrection of Jesus would guarantee life from the dead for evermore for all who look to him. We will see this comparison in another context shortly.

Another feature, which we will also see in the next example, is the fact that Moses was only the guide to the healing object, which in this case was the brass serpent. But Jesus *himself* is the source of salvation to all who obey him. He was the one lifted up on the cross as the healing source for all sinners bound in their transgressions. The effective instrument was the brass serpent which is a type of Christ. Moses was only God's agent for directing the Israelites towards it.

2. The Bread of Life

The next example is found in the sixth chapter of John's Gospel. The chapter begins with the miracle of Jesus in feeding five thousand men, besides women and children, from only five barley loaves and two fish (John 6:9). The crowds were astonished and sought to make Jesus their king, but he withdrew from them (v.15). The next day they sought for Jesus and finally found him on the other side of the Sea of Galilee. Jesus was aware that they were only seeking him because of the miracle he had performed and warned them "not to labour for the food which perishes but for the food which endures to eternal life" which he, the Son of man, would give to them (v.27). They replied:

> Then what sign do you do, that we may see, and believe you? What work do you perform? Our fathers ate the manna in the wilderness; as it is written, He gave them bread from heaven to eat.
> *John 6:30-31*

Jesus responded that it was not Moses who gives the true bread from heaven but his Father who is in heaven, bread which comes down from heaven to give life to the world. When the appealed to him to give them this bread always, he answered:

> I am the bread of life; he who comes to me shall not hunger, and he who believes in me shall never thirst. John 6:35

Once again John draws out a sharp contrast between Jesus and Moses. Moses, again, was only God's agent to bring down the manna from heaven that fed the Israelites for forty years, but Jesus *himself* is the true bread of life which comes down from heaven. It's the same contrast that we saw in the comparison with the brass serpent. So also is the comparison Jesus brings between the temporal nature of Moses' miracle and the eternal effects of his own provision of himself as the bread of life. When the Jews alluded to the miracle of Moses in the desert, what they were doing was to throw down the gauntlet to Jesus. He had fed more than five thousand of them with just a few loaves. Sure, that was an incredible miracle, but how did he compare with Moses who had done the same thing for forty years? Jesus had also had something to work with, five loaves and two fish, but Moses had brought the manna down to earth from heaven with nothing in his hands. Could Jesus perform similar miracles?

The Jews appeared to have conveniently forgot what their forefathers' impression was of the manna. "We loathe this worthless food," they declared (Numbers 21:5). Nonetheless what Jesus proceeded to do was not to claim that his bread was of a better quality than Moses' manna. It was the ultimate effect of them both that was the issue. He said to them:

> I am the bread of life. Your fathers ate the manna in the wilderness and they died. This is the bread which comes down from heaven that a man may eat of it and not die. I am the living bread which came down from heaven; if anyone eats of this bread, he will live for ever; and the bread which I shall give for the life of the world is my flesh. *John 6:48-51*

Here again we see the superiority of Jesus over Moses. He himself is the bread of life and, unlike the Israelites who perished in the wilderness despite eating the manna for forty years, whoever feeds on this bread will live for ever. These are powerful sources for witness to Muslims of the glory of Jesus over Moses and his supreme purpose for coming to earth - to bring eternal salvation to all who come to him and believe in him.

3. Healing a Man's Whole Body

The third example is found in the next chapter. The Jews in Judea had been looking for Jesus, wondering if he would come up to the feast of Tabernacles. Many opposed his teaching, especially because he had been known to heal people on the sabbath day which, to their knowledge, was a contravention of the law of Moses. So Jesus said to them:

> If on the sabbath a man receives circumcision, so that the law of Moses may not be broken, are you angry with me because on the sabbath I made a man's whole body well? *John 7:23*

The Jews did not believe they were breaking the sabbath when they applied the covenantal law of circumcision. Yet that is all that it was, merely a ritual to bind an Israelite male child to the national covenant God had made with them through Moses. Jesus, however, had done far more. During his previous trip to Jerusalem he had healed a man who had been lame and paralysed for thirty-eight years (John 5:9). Here, once again, we see the superiority of Jesus over Moses. Circumcision affected only an organ of the body. Jesus had made the lame man's *whole body* well.

4. The Woman Caught in Adultery

Our fourth example is the occasion where the Jews brought to Jesus a woman who had been caught in the act of adultery. They charged him: "Now in the law Moses commanded us to stone such. What do you say about her?" (John 8:5). They aimed to catch him however he answered. If he showed his customary compassion to the woman, they would accuse him of undermining the law of Moses. If he agreed with them, however, they would have handed him a stone and told him, as the one who had pronounced judgment on her, to cast the first stone. Jesus answered them:

> Let him who is without sin among you be the first to throw a stone at her. *John 8:7*

They went out, one by one, till Jesus was left with the woman standing alone before him. Under the law of Moses she stood condemned as a sinner for her specific breach of the seventh commandment. Under the light of Christ, however, they all went out convicted of their sin. After pardoning the woman Jesus said to them: "I am the light of the world, he who follows me will not walk in darkness, but will have the light of life" (v.12). He was the true light, which enlightens ever man, who had come into the world. His influence was more universal than the law of Moses.

5. The Blind Man

The last example is the man who was blind from his birth whom Jesus healed on another sabbath day (John 9:14). As usual the Pharisees murmured against him because they did not believe people should be healed on the sabbath. When they challenged the man who had formerly been blind he simply recounted how Jesus had anointed his eyes with clay and, when he had washed them, received his sight. They pressed their case on him, declaring that they knew Jesus to be a sinner. He replied that he could not answer whether he was a sinner or not. Once he was blind, and now he could see. When he asked the Pharisees whether they also wanted to become disciples of Jesus, they replied:

> You are his disciple, but we are disciples of Moses. We know that God has spoken to Moses, but as for this man, we do not know where he comes from. *John 9:28-29*

The man answered that this was a marvel. Jesus had opened his eyes no sinner could do this with the power of God. He concluded with these significant words:

> Never since the world began has it been heard that any one opened the eyes of a man born blind. If this man were not from God, he could do nothing. *John 9:32-33*

Here again John points out the superiority of Jesus over Moses. No one, not even Moses, had ever given sight to a man blind from his birth.

These miracles were unsurpassed in Israelite history. They pointed to Jesus as a much greater man than all the prophets who came before him. He was not just a messenger, he was the message itself - the one through whom God's saving grace for all mankind would be achieved.

Christians have important material in all these comparisons in their witness to Muslims to show that Jesus was not just an ordinary prophet. He came as the saviour, the promised Messiah, the Son of God, to complete God's final work on earth - the reconciliation of all men, Muslims included, to God through his death and resurrection.

David

Prophecies of Death and Resurrection

The Crucifixion of Jesus foretold in Psalm 22

One of the most remarkable, indeed overwhelming, evidences of the truth of the Christian faith is the many predictions of the crucifixion and resurrection of Jesus Christ in passages of the Old Testament dating up to a thousand years before the event. There are two Psalms which we will look at in this chapter where both are foretold. We will begin with those that foretell the crucifixion. Psalm 22, one of the greatest Messianic psalms, will be the first example. It begins:

> My God, my God, why have you forsaken me? Why are you so far from helping me, from the words of my groaning?
>
> *Psalm 22:1*

The psalm is a unique one. It is one of the psalms of David, yet it touches distress, even to death, in a way the great shepherd-king of Israel could never have personally known. The first words have an echo in the only outcry of Jesus from the cross mentioned in the Gospels of Matthew and Mark. In the midst of the crucifixion, at the depth of his despair, he cried out "Eli, Eli, lama sabach-thani," meaning the same as the first words of the psalm, "My God, my God, why have you forsaken me" (Matthew 27: 46, Mark 15:34). Jesus would have known the words of the Old Testament text, but it is hardly likely that he was merely repeating them from memory. He *cried out* from the depth of his eternal soul, and the cry was one which has been described as the strangest which ever went from earth to heaven.

This was the only time Jesus ever prayed "My God, my God." On all other occasions he called out "My Father" (Matthew 26:42), or just "Father" (John 12:28), or spoke of him as the "heavenly Father" (Matthew 5:48, Luke 11:13). At this one moment, one of the holiest and most sacred in all human history, he could only cry "My God." At no point in all history did the Son of God look less like the image of his Father in his eternal glory. More importantly, there was never a time when he felt so cut off and forcibly separated from Him, yet at no other time was the wondrous love of the Father for his followers more splendidly revealed than at this point when both Father and Son endured the anguish and intense pain of separation from each other.

This first verse of Psalm 22 is holy ground and Muslims need to be brought reverently to see its implications. It sets the tone for the rest of the psalm. We will look at particular verses in it that have New Testament parallels. The next text is this one:

> All who see me mock at me, they make mouths at me, they wag their heads; "He committed his cause to the Lord; let him deliver him, let him rescue him, for he delights in him."
>
> *Psalm 22:8*

The chief priests who stood at the foot of the cross thought they had finally gained their victory over Jesus. As he hung there, helpless, they unwittingly fulfilled the words of this very text when they mocked Jesus and declared:

> He saved others, he cannot save himself. He is the King of Israel; let him come down now from the cross, and we will believe in him. He trusts in God; let God deliver him now, if he desires him, for he said "I am the Son of God". *Matthew 27:42-43*

This is just one instance where you can show Muslims that predictions about the crucifixion of Jesus were fulfilled to the letter a thousand years later. David continues with these words:

> I am poured out like water, and all my bones are out of joint; my heart is like wax, it is melted within my breast; my strength is dried up like a potsherd, and my tongue cleaves to my jaws, you lay me in the dust of death. *Psalm 22:14-15*

This is a perfect description of the anguish of a man being crucified, yet crucifixion was unknown during the time of David. He goes on "They have pierced my hands and feet" (v.16), another specific anticipation of the crucifixion. This psalm is not merely an expression of David's anguish in a time of trouble, it is a remarkable anticipation of the crucifixion of the Messiah, the eternal Son of David, to follow. One verse particularly stands out in the psalm:

> They divide my garments among them, and for my raiment they cast lots. *Psalm 22:18*

It is not immediately obvious that this is a striking riddle, an exception to the usual style of Hebrew poetry. For the sake of emphasis the same point is often made in Hebrew poetical texts in different words which basically have the same meaning. For example: "Your name, O Lord, endures for ever, your renown, O Lord, throughout all ages" (Psalm 35:13). "Name" and "renown" are synonyms, as are "for ever" and "throughout all ages." The Psalms are saturated with this form of expression. Psalm 22:18, however, is a strange exception. Garments and raiment are synonyms, they are both descriptions for general clothing. Yet "divide" and "cast lots" are antonyms, opposite terms with expressly different meanings.

No Hebrew could ever have worked this riddle out, especially in its unique form of speech. To divide means to separate, but to cast lots means to keep the garment together. What could this have meant? How could they cast lots for his garment, yet at the same time separate it? It seems like a contradiction. For ten centuries no Hebrew scholar could possibly have given the answer, but a simple explanation appears in this brief narrative about the way the Roman soldiers handled the clothing of Jesus at the foot of his cross:

> When the soldiers had crucified Jesus they took his garments and made four parts, one for each soldier; also his tunic. But the tunic was without seam, woven from top to bottom; so they said to one another, "Let us not tear it, but cast lots for it to see whose it shall be." *John 19:23-24*

Now the riddle finally makes sense. The soldiers cast lots for the tunic Jesus had worn but divided his other garments among them. John expressly says that this simple activity of the Roman soldiers was a direct fulfilment of Psalm 22:18 (John 19:24). The soldiers could hardly have been aware that they were directly fulfilling a prophecy made a thousand years earlier.

We will return to the psalm, but at this point you can see how effectively you can witness to the crucifixion of Jesus through specific predictions made centuries earlier. Not just one prediction but many are made in detail in the first twenty-one verses of the psalm. It's a tremendous source of convincing proofs of the crucifixion event.

Similar Prophecies in Psalm 69

A very similar psalm of David, Psalm 69, also contains a number of specific predictions of the crucifixion, some in fine detail. It begins:

> I am weary with my crying; my throat is parched. My eyes grow dim with waiting for my God. More in number than the hairs of my head are those who hate me without cause. *Psalm 69:3-4*

The dryness in his throat is another typical experience of a man crucified. Once again we behold a victim in terrible distress as his life ebbs away. Jesus applied the following words to himself, saying:

> Now they have seen and hated both me and my Father. It is to fulfil the word that is written in their law, "they hated me without a cause." *John 15:25*

Here again you have specific material to show Muslims that the crucifixion, which the Qur'an denies (Surah 4:157), was specifically predicted in great detail in the Psalms (Zabur) of David a thousand years earlier. David proceeds, in his own anguish, to confess his folly and wrongdoings (v.5) which Jesus would take on himself on the cross, but the whole unfolding drama again takes on Messianic dimensions in these words:

> For it is for your sake that I have borne reproach, that shame has covered my face. *Psalm 69:7*

The Apostle Paul also applies these words directly to Jesus when he says:

> For Christ did not please himself; but, as it is written, "The reproaches of those who reproached you have fallen on me."
> *Romans 15:3*

The next text also has a direct sequel in the life of Jesus: "For zeal for your house has consumed me" (Psalm 69:9). When Jesus drove the moneychangers out of the Temple and poured out their coins, overturning their tables, and told the Jews not to make his Father's house a house of trade, his disciples remembered that it was written "zeal for your house will consume me" (John 2:17).

The Psalm continues with growing cries of anguish as the victim nears his death. "I am in distress," he cries (v.17), "I am in despair. I looked for pity but there was none, and for comforters, but I found none" (v.20).

Then comes another very specific statement which has a remarkable fulfilment at the foot of Jesus' cross:

> They gave me poison for food, and for my thirst they gave me vinegar to drink. *Psalm 69:21*

When Jesus cried out from the cross "I thirst" (John 19:28), a bowl of vinegar stood next to the cross, "so they put a sponge full of vinegar on hyssop and held it to his mouth" (v.29). It is amazing to see how many predictions of the crucifixion were fulfilled in such detail when Jesus died. Christians have emphatic proofs of the truth of the death of Jesus on the cross in these exceptional passages. Psalm 69:25 is also quoted in Acts 1:20 as a deliberate prediction of the desolate end of Judas Iscariot for betraying Jesus. It is very useful, in Muslim homes, to go slowly through both psalms (22 and 69) and to draw Muslims to the very experience of the Son of God as he hung there that fateful Friday.

Both psalms bring the agony to a climax as the suffering victim finally breathes his last and expires. The first concludes the anguish in these heart-rending cries:

> Deliver my soul from the sword, my life from the power of the dog! Save me from the mouth of the lion, my afflicted soul from the horns of the wild oxen! *Psalm 22:20-21*

The second also builds up to a crescendo as the distress and suffering reach their peak. The psalmist cries out " But I am afflicted and in pain; let your salvation, O God, set me on high" (Psalm 69:29). There the anguish ends in both psalms, yet the narrative goes on. The tone changes, the confidence returns, and in perfect health the sufferer praises God for his redemption from the pit.

The Resurrection of Jesus in Both Psalms

Not only is the crucifixion of Jesus foretold in these two psalms but we also find clear evidences of his resurrection as well. As we have seen, Jesus cried out to his Father on the cross in the exact words Psalm 22 begins with, "My God, my God, why have you forsaken me?" The psalm then covers the anguish and pain of a man in great distress, who had committed his cause to the Lord, and who prayed to him for deliverance. The suffering part of the psalm reaches a final crescendo in the heart-rending cries, "O Lord, be not far off! Hasten to my aid! Deliver my soul from the sword. Save my afflicted soul!" (vs 19-21). Suddenly the tone of the psalm changes:

> I will tell of your name to my brethren; in the midst of the congregation I will praise you. From you comes my praise in the great congregation; my vows I will pay before those who fear him.
>
> *Psalm 22:22,25*

There is a dramatic change here, an immediate transformation. Now the psalmist speaks confidently, resolutely, triumphantly, and with complete composure. He has triumphed over his affliction. He calls on all true believers to praise God, to glorify him and stand in awe of him. For, he declares, the Lord has not hid his face from his affliction but has heard when he cried to him! (Psalm 22:23-24). The rest of the Psalm follows the same pattern - triumph, praise and complete composure. The afflicted one, whose anguish increased to the point of total desolation, is now delivered!

The resurrection of Jesus is the scene foreshadowed in the second part of the psalm. No one reading the whole song can miss the sharp contrast between the victim's growing, intensifying anguish (vs 1-21), and the victor's glory and triumph (vs 22-31). It is a vivid picture of the crucifixion and resurrection of Jesus. You can point out to Muslims that the words of Psalm 22:22 quoted above are expressly applied to Jesus in Hebrews 2:12. You may not be able to work through this line of witness with obstinate Muslims who will seek only to ridicule and refute everything you say, but with seeking Muslims whose eyes and hearts are opened, this subject is a powerful witness of the fact that Jesus Christ is the ultimate figurehead, God's chosen Messiah, whose death and resurrection were not only prophesied but revealed in the deep, personal emotions that he was destined to experience, no less than a thousand years before these great events occurred.

Psalm 69 follows the exact same pattern, not out of coincidence, but divine intention. Once again the first part of the psalm (vs 1-29) follows the same pattern of victimisation, leading up to a climax of suffering and anguish. The theme stands out: "Save me, O God! I am in distress. Draw near to me, redeem me. Set me free! I am afflicted and in pain. Let your salvation, O God, set me on high!" (vs 1,17,18,29). Suddenly, as in Psalm 22, the tone and setting change dramatically. Victimisation gives way to victory. The lamb becomes the lion:

> I will praise the name of God with a song; I will magnify him with thanksgiving. Let heaven and earth praise him, the seas and everything that moves therein. *Psalm 69:30,34*

Once again it is a song of praise, in complete composure, in the dawn of victory, that characterises the remaining verses of the psalm (vs 30-36). The suffering servant has become the risen deliverer! Anguish has given way to triumph! Jesus Christ has risen from the dead! Yet the passage in the psalms chosen by the disciples of Jesus more than any other to prove that the resurrection of Jesus from the dead was foretold a millennium earlier is this one:

> I keep the Lord always before me; because he is at my right hand, I shall not be moved. Therefore my heart is glad, and my soul rejoices; my body also dwells secure. For you do not give me up to Sheol, or let your godly one see the pit. You do show me the path of life; in your presence there is fulness of joy, in your right hand are pleasures for evermore. *Psalm 16:8-11*

Once again this is a psalm of David, but the New Testament aggressively takes it away from him and applies it directly to the person of Jesus Christ. On the day of Pentecost, just after the Holy Spirit had been poured out upon the disciples so that they faced the whole Jewish nation with confidence and assurance, Simon Peter declared that, even though they had crucified Jesus by the hands of lawless men, God has raised him from the dead, having loosed the pangs of death, because he could not be held by them (Acts 2:23-24). He then went on to quote this same passage from Psalm 16 and, when he had finished, he declared that everyone knew that Davis had died, was buried, and that the site of his tomb was well known. So he could not be speaking of himself but, knowing that God had sworn to him with an oath that one of his descendants would sit on his throne for all eternity, "he foresaw and spoke of the resurrection of the Christ," that he did not go down to Sheol, nor did his flesh see corruption (Acts 2:29-31). Peter then concluded:

> This Jesus God raised up, and of that we are all witnesses. *Acts 2:32*

Going on to quote Psalm 110:1 ("The Lord said to my Lord, Sit at my right hand, till I make your enemies a stool for your feet"), he added that David had not descended into heaven and so, in this declaration, foretold the ascension of the Christ, the same Jesus whom they had now betrayed and crucified (Acts 2:34-36).

In all these passages from the Psalms, you have tremendous material to show Muslims that the crucifixion, resurrection and ascension to heaven were foretold by David in his Psalms a thousand years before the events happened. Not only were they predicted, but they were outlined in such fine detail that the deepest emotions of the Christ were even set out in such detail that you could know exactly what he was experiencing within his eternal soul.

The Deity of Jesus Christ in the Psalms

The fact that Jesus is the eternal Son of God is also foretold in the Psalms of David. Nothing, it appears, was overlooked. The evidences are there for all to see and are sufficient to convince any sincere seeker of the truth. There is, quite simply, no ambiguity in this declaration:

> I will tell of the decree of the Lord: He said to me, "You are my Son, today I have begotten you. Ask of me, and I will make the nations your heritage, and the ends of the earth your possession."
> *Psalm 2:7-8*

We are not speculating when we apply this passage to the Lord Jesus Christ (there hardly appears to be a contender for its application!). The Apostle Paul deliberately applied this text to Jesus in his sermon to the Jews who were gathered together in the synagogue at Antioch in Pisidia on the sabbath day (Acts 13:33). To what angel, another New Testament text enquires, did God ever say "You are my Son, today I have begotten you"? (Hebrews 1:5). The immediately succeeding verses are also applied to Jesus in Acts 4:25-26.

Perhaps the most moving and descriptive passage incorporating a prediction of the deity of the son of David to come is found in another psalm. It begins with these words:

> Of old you spoke in a vision to your faithful one, and said: "I have set the crown upon one who is mighty, I have exalted one chosen from the people." *Psalm 89:19*

The next verse specifically applies this prophecy to David himself but, like the others we have considered, it soon becomes obvious that this is a double-barrelled prophecy and ultimately applies to the descendant of David to come, who would rule over the throne of God forever, and whom the Jesus would subsequently call the son of David. God speaks and says of this great Messiah to come:

> My faithfulness and my steadfast love will be with him, and in my name shall his horn be exalted. I will set his hand on the sea and his right hand on the rivers. *Psalm 89:24-25*

Once again we hear words of triumph and victory as the Son of God, who became the Son of man, takes his eternal throne and establishes complete authority over all the earth. The declaration reaches its climax, and identifies the one of whom it speaks, in these words:

> He shall cry to me, "You are my Father, my God and the Rock of my salvation." And I will make him the first-born, the highest of the kings of earth. My steadfast love I will keep for him forever, and my covenant will stand firm for him. I will establish his line for ever and his throne as the days of the heavens.
>
> *Psalm 89:25-29*

The Qur'an does not say much about David. He is seen as one of the great patriarchs and prophets of old and some Biblical narratives about him are repeated in a somewhat disjointed fashion in the book. But it does say of him:

> We strengthened his kingdom, and gave him wisdom and sound judgment in speech and decision.
>
> *Surah 38:20*

These words are only a shadow of the Christ whose coming, crucifixion, death, resurrection, ascension to glory, and eternal deity David foretold. In these great predictions, hundreds of years before they came to pass, Christians have more than sufficient material to witness to Muslims of who Jesus Christ really was and why he came to earth. God has left us a persuasive record in the songs of David of the Son of God to come, who would cry to him as both his God and Father, and to whom all authority over earth and the heavens would ultimately be given.

Solomon

Image of the True Son of David

The Son of David, The Son of God

The Qur'an does not speak much of Solomon. It sees him as a Prophet of God who possessed great power (Surah 2.102), to whom great understanding and wisdom had been given so that he could judge righteously (Surah 21.79), for whom the wind did obeisance and a molten brass flowed (Surah 34.12), and who prayed that a kingdom which should be his eternally, should be given to him (Surah 38.35). The only lengthy passage devoted to Solomon sees him as a great ruler who had been taught the speech of birds so that he could even hold a conversation with a hoopoe, who had a host of jinns (ordinary spirits, most of whom were demons, but some believers) doing service to him. It also has a somewhat disjointed account of his meeting with the Queen of Sheba. No biography of Solomon, such as we find in the Bible, can possibly be derived from these passages and we are left with a somewhat incoherent account of his life and leadership.

In witnessing to Muslims we need not compare this deficient record with the very well ordered account of his life in the Bible. We could go into some detail to show how his forty-year rule over Israel developed but we would be doing no more than to fill in the gaps. There is one supreme role that he played that we are interested in, and that we would want to commend to Muslims, and that is his foreshadowing of the eternal kingdom of the greater Son of David to come, namely Jesus Christ.

The Old Testament contains one particular passage that the religious leaders and, indeed, the whole nation of Israel in coming generations, believed to be a prophecy of a great Messianic figure to come who would reign over the house of David for ever. David, the greatest of the prophet-kings of Israel, determined one day to build a majestic temple for the God of Israel, a house for his ark to dwell in, so that the nation would honour him as their sole Lord and Deliverer. God told his servant Nathan, in return to remind David that he had never asked for a temple built of cedar to dwell in (1 Chronicles 17:5), but, he declared, he would build a house in return for him. This is what he specifically promised:

> When your days are fulfilled to go to be with your fathers, I will raise up your offspring after you, one of your own sons, and I will establish his kingdom. He shall build a house for me, and I will establish his throne for ever. I will be his father, and he shall be my son; I will not take my steadfast love from him, as I took it from him who was before you, but I will confirm him in my house and in my kingdom for ever and his throne shall be established for ever.
>
> *1 Chronicles 17:11-14*

For forty years after David's death Solomon ruled over the house of Israel in peace. Israel, for this brief period, became the strongest nation in the region. Even her enemies were at peace with her. It was a time of unparalleled prosperity and the nation's security seemed assured. God's covenant with Israel finally seemed established. Yet, before his death, Solomon took many foreign wives and allowed the nation to become corrupted with pagan practices. On his death Israel split into two rival groups, Israel and Judah, under Jeroboam and Rehoboam respectively, who warred with each other incessantly. A succession of evil kings led the Israelites into paganism, Baal-worship and degradation until they were taken into exile in Assyria. Judah endured a mixture of righteous and evil kings but eventually, she too became corrupted and was taken into exile in Babylon. The temple of Solomon was destroyed and the land lay desolate. The nation knew that Solomon, although bearing many of the marks of the promised Son to come, could not have been the true Son of David who was promised. The nation looked to an eternal ruler still to come whom they named the Messiah, the ultimate Son of David.

When Jesus began his ministry nearly a thousand years later, the nation was eagerly looking for this greater Son of David who would rule over the house of David for ever. Could Jesus be him? (John 7:26). When he entered Jerusalem for the last time before his crucifixion Jesus engaged in a comprehensive debate with the Jews one day during which they pestered him with many questions. When they were finally exhausted he asked them just one question in return. The narrative reads:

> Now while the Pharisees were gathered together, Jesus asked them a question, saying "What do you think of the Christ? Whose son is

he?" They said to him "The son of David." He said to them, How is it then that David, inspired by the Spirit, calls him Lord, saying "The Lord said to my Lord, Sit at my right hand, till I put your enemies under your feet." If David thus calls him Lord, how is he his son?." *Matthew 22:41-45*

The Jews may have missed the point, but you can make it very effectively with Muslims. God had promised *"I* will be his *Father*, and he shall be *my Son*". Solomon was only a type of the greater Son of David to come who would also be the Son of God. This is why David called him his Lord. Here, a thousand years before he was born, you have proof that the coming Messiah would be the Son of God and that his Father would give him a kingdom and throne to last for ever. This passage strengthens the similar passage we quoted in the last chapter, namely Psalm 89:19-28, where David himself sees the coming of the same Messiah whom he foreshadowed, who would cry to God "You are my Father" and to whom a throne would be given which would last "as the days of the heavens". How could the Messiah be both the Son of David and his Lord, Jesus asked? The answer is given in these words from Jesus himself::

I am the root and the offspring of David, the bright morning star. *Revelation 22:16*

Here is much material for your witness to Muslims. Being descended from David, Jesus was his offspring, but being his Lord from all eternity, he was also his root. This explains the role of Solomon as a type of the Son of God. He ruled over a kingdom that was undisturbed in its peace and prosperity for forty years. In this he foreshadowed the eternal rule of the Son of God to come. Solomon was a type of the Son of God.

The Second Coming: Christ in His Glory

There is still more to this than first meets the eye. Solomon was not only a type of the Christ, the greater Son of David, the Son of God to come. He also prefigures the *second coming* of Jesus, and that in a very clearly defined context. The first verse of the New Testament reveals this context:

The book of the genealogy of Jesus Christ, the son of David, the son of Abraham. *Matthew 1:1*

We have already seen how Isaac, the son of the great patriarch Abraham, prefigured the first coming of Jesus. His unique birth, his sacrifice, and his father's belief that he would be raised from the ashed, foreshadowed the life of Jesus to come in his first coming to earth. Solomon represents the second coming of Jesus, especially in his role as the undisputed king of Israel in an undisturbed period of Israel's history, indeed its highest point. Son of the great patriarch David, he prefigures the glorious reign of Jesus to come when he will rule unchallenged over the house of God for ever. You can use the following comparisons to make the point to Muslims:

1. Solomon's reign was one of undisturbed peace

At no other time did Israel enjoy such peace and prosperity as it did in the days of Solomon. This verse emphasises this precious period in the nation's history:

> And Judah and Israel dwelt in safety, from Dan even to Beersheba, every man under his vine and under his fig tree, all the days of Solomon. *1 Kings 4:25*

The eternal reign of Jesus will also be one of lasting peace. "Death shall be no more, neither shall there be mourning nor crying nor pain anymore, for the former things have passed away" (Revelation 21:4).

2. Even Israel's enemies were at peace with her

When Hiram, the king of Tyre, heard that Solomon reigned over the nation of Israel in place of his father David, he sent his servants to hin in peace, for he had loved David. Solomon reminded him that God had promised his father David that his son would build a house for his name, so he requested Hiram to command that the choicest cedars of Lebanon should be cut down for the temple he was about to build (1 Kings 5:1-6). Hiram responded gladly and gave him all the cedar and cypress timber that he required. "And there was peace between Hiram and Solomon; and the two of them made a treaty" (1 Kings 5:12).

The forty-year reign in complete peace and the building of the house of God by David's son represents the eternal reign of peace that Jesus will bring when he, the Son of God, rules over the house of God for ever. These verses express this theme perfectly:

> He shall command peace to the nations; his dominion shall be from sea to sea, and from the River to the ends of the earth.
> *Zechariah 9:10*

Of the increase of his government and of peace there will be no end. *Isaiah 9:7*

3. Solomon's temple represents the eternal kingdom

Before his throne Solomon made a molten sea. It was round and stood on twelve oxen, three facing each direction (east, west, north and south). Its thickness was a handbreath, yet it held two thousand baths (1 Kings 7:23-26). John, in his vision of the eternal kingdom, saw a similar picture:

> And I saw what appeared to be a sea of glass mingled with fire, and those who had conquered the beast and its image and the number of its name, standing beside the sea of glass with the harps of God in their hands. *Revelation 15:2*

4. Solomon drew the worshippers toward Jerusalem

When his temple was completed Solomon prayed to God that wherever his people might be, even caught in their sins and carried away captive by their enemies to a foreign land, they might turn towards the temple and be remembered by God:

> If they repent with all their mind and with all their heart in the land of their enemies, who carried them captive, and pray to you toward their land, which you gave to their fathers, the city which you have chosen, and the house which I have built for your name; then hear in heaven, your dwelling place, their prayer and their supplication, and maintain their cause, and forgive your people who have sinned against you. *1 Kings 8:48-50*

Jesus expressed much the same longing and concern when he cried out over the same temple mount in Jerusalem, "How often would I have gathered your children together as a hen gathers her brood under wings, and you would not! Behold, your house is forsaken and desolate" (Matthew 23: 37-38).

5. The glory of Solomon's rule

Solomon eventually excelled all the kings of the earth in riches and wisdom. "And the whole earth sought the presence of Solomon to hear his wisdom which God had put into his mind. Every one of them brought his present, articles of silver and gold, garments, myrrh, spices, horses and mules, so much year by year" (1 Kings 10:23-25).

Speaking of himself Jesus said "The queen of the south came from the ends of the earth to hear the wisdom of Solomon, and behold, something greater than Solomon is here" (Matthew 12:42). When he returns at his second coming he will introduce a kingdom with unparalleled splendour. "The kings of the earth shall bring their glory into it ... they shall bring into it the glory and honour of the nations" (Revelation 21:24,26). The walls of the kingdom will be built of jasper while the city will be pure gold, clear as glass. Its foundations will be adorned with every jewel: jasper, sapphire, agate, emerald, onyx, carnelian, chrysolite, beryl, topaz, chrysoprase, jacinth and amethyst (Revelation 21:19-20).

Solomon's temple and kingdom were a type of the glory of Jesus to come when, at his second coming, he will introduce his eternal kingdom in all its glory and splendour, over which he will reign for ever and ever. You have much rich material here for witness to Muslims. Yet another great prophet of God, named in the Qur'an, can be called as a witness to the glory of the Christian Gospel.

Isaiah

Behold the Servant He has Chosen

The Great Messianic Prophecies

The Qur'an makes no mention of the prophet Isaiah, one of the greatest of the Old Testament prophets. In fact the book knows none of his generation. Ezekiel, Jeremiah and the minor prophets, together with Isaiah, were a group of great prophets of a specific age in Israel's history when the climactic vision of God's final purpose for his people began to unfold. The only prophet of this time mentioned in the Qur'an is Jonah, significantly the only prophet whose book is a narrative of his unique experiences, especially his three days in the stomach of a large fish. All the others follow the same pattern. They are oracles of God's anger against an ever-rebellious nation with warnings of the judgments to come upon it coupled with unique promises of a golden, Messianic age to come when God's purposes would be fulfilled.

Yet it is in these passages in the Bible that we find some of the best materials for witnessing to Muslims of who Jesus Christ really was and what he was sent to accomplish on earth. You have here some of the most emphatic proofs in the scriptures of his deity and redeeming work, written up to seven hundred years before the events they describe and foretell. Two verses testify to his deity, the first of which is:

> Therefore the Lord himself will give you a sign. Behold, a young woman shall conceive and bear a son, and shall call his name Immanuel. *Isaiah 7:14*

In the Greek Septuagint the word almah in Hebrew, meaning young woman, is translated as *bethulah*, meaning "a virgin." The translation is obviously correct. The sign to be given to the nation is that a young virgin, too young to have married or borne children, would conceive by the power of God and bear a son. No ordinary son, mind you, but the Son of God himself. Immanuel he would be called, meaning "God is with us." This verse is quoted in Matthew 1:23 as a deliberate proof that the unique birth of Jesus Christ, born of the virgin Mary, was foretold no less than seven hundred years before it occurred.

Muslims freely believe in the virgin-birth of Jesus as it is mentioned in the Qur'an in the same emphatic language as it is in the Bible (Surah 3:47-49, 19:19-22). The Qur'an, however, misses the essential point. It is because he is the Son of God that he was born of a virgin. He had existed from all eternity and could not possibly be conceived by the normal means of human procreation. This is precisely what the Angel Gabriel testified at his conception when he said to Mary his mother:

> The Holy Spirit will come upon you, and the power of the Most High will overshadow you; therefore the child to be born will be called holy, the Son of God. *Luke 2:35*

A similar, equally famous, passage from the book of Isaiah confirms the announcement that the great Messiah to come would not be just an ordinary human being but would have the very presence of the divine being dwelling within him. The passage reads:

> For to us a child is born, to us a son is given; and the government will be upon his shoulder, and his name will be called "Wonderful Counsellor, Mighty God, Everlasting Father, Prince of Peace." Of the increase of his government and of peace there will be no end, upon the throne of David, and over his kingdom, to establish it, and to uphold it with justice and with righteousness from this time forth and for evermore. Isaiah 9:6-7

A son is promised - being no one less than the Son of God. The titles and description of this son make it clear that he is a divine being. His kingdom will last for eternity, the paragraph testifies, once again emphasising the presence of the eternal God within the soul of this great human Deliverer to come. It is almost incredible to see the identity of the eternal Son of God, Jesus Christ, foreshadowed in these great prophecies made long before his time.

In your witness to Muslims you can also impress on them the fact that Isaiah is a Jewish scripture from their holy book, which we call the Old Testament, written centuries before it came to pass. As the Jews have always disowned the possibility that God could have a Son (just as the Muslims do), it is striking to find such predictions in their own texts, where the very divinity of the eternal Son to come is undeniably prestated, in view of their denial of what they teach. This is no interpolated Christian scripture. Two scrolls of Isaiah were found among the Dead Sea Scrolls dating back to before the time of Jesus, yet they include these very same prophecies that could only have had one fulfilment.

Further Messianic Prophecies from Isaiah

Another well-known passage from the book of Isaiah follows. It is worth quoting the whole text because it is freely quoted in the New Testament. It reads:

> There shall come forth a shoot from the stump of Jesse, and a branch shall grow out of his roots. And the Spirit of the Lord shall rest upon him, the spirit of wisdom and understanding, the spirit of counsel and might, the spirit of knowledge and fear of the Lord. And his delight shall be in the fear of the Lord. He shall not judge by what his eyes see, or decide by what his ears hear; but with righteousness he shall judge the poor, and decide with equity for the meek of the earth; and he shall smite the earth with the rod of his mouth, and with the breath of his lips he shall slay the wicked. Righteousness shall be the girdle of his waist, and faithfulness the girdle of his loins. *Isaiah 11:1-5*

By the time of Jesus' birth the line of Jesse through his son David had indeed become no more than a stump. The Son of God was born in humility of a family line that had all but lost its glorious past, yet the birth of this great Saviour, upon whom the Spirit of the Lord would rest (as it did at his baptism - Matthew 3:16), was the fulfilment of this great vision of one, supreme, divine Deliverer to come. This passage is a dramatic description of both the humility and the glory of the divine Messiah to come. It recognises his meekness and gentleness at his first coming, and his authority and rule to follow with his second coming thereafter.

A very similar passage, promising the advent of one great servant of God yet to come, is found later in the book of Isaiah. It reads:

> Behold my servant, whom I uphold, my chosen, in whom my soul delights; I have put my Spirit upon him, he will bring forth justice to the nations. He will not cry or lift up his voice, or make it heard in the street; a bruised read he will not break, and a dimly burning

> wick he will not quench; he will faithfully bring forth justice.
> *Isaiah 42:1-4*

Once again God speaks of his great servant to come. This passage is quoted in full in Matthew 12:18-20 and is applied directly to Jesus Christ. Christians witnessing to Muslims have, here, substantial proof of the fact that Jesus (and, by inference, not Muhammad) was the great figurehead, the final climactic Deliverer to come, whose advent was foretold on so many occasions by the great prophet Isaiah. One last passage, very similar to the two we have quoted, settles the emphasis on the great Messiah, God's eternal Saviour, to come. It reads:

> The Spirit of the Lord God is upon me, because the Lord has anointed me to bring good tidings to the afflicted, he has sent me to bind up the brokenhearted, to proclaim liberty to the captives, and the opening of the prison to those who are bound; to proclaim the year of the Lord's favour. *Isaiah 61:1-2*

This passage is also quoted in the New Testament in full, but in a much more expressive context (Luke 4:18-19). It is not just applied to Jesus by one of the Gospel writers - Jesus applied the passage to himself one day as he read it in a synagogue in Nazareth. The very locality is significant. For thirty years the townsfolk of Nazareth had known him as one of them without ever suspecting he was the one promised in all these emphatic prophetic narratives. He was given a scroll of the book of Isaiah to read that sabbath morning and specifically looked for this passage. Once he had found it and had read it out, he closed the book, gave it to the attendant alongside him, and declared:

> Today this scripture has been fulfilled in your hearing.
> *Luke 4:21*

The crowd spoke well of him and wondered at the gracious words that proceeded from his mouth, but they soon took exception to him, remembering that he was, in their view, just another ordinary member of their community. An altercation and argument followed which ended with Jesus walking away from them, but the die had been cast. This incident happened very early in his ministry and is a bold confirmation that he was the servant of God, the unique Saviour, whose coming had been prophesied in so many of the oracles of Isaiah the prophet.

You can, in an evening's discussion with receptive Muslims, show them from this passage and all the others quoted here that it was the coming of Jesus that the nation of Israel was told to anticipate, and that he was to come as their great Deliverer and Redeemer. His divinity, meekness, gentleness, and yet ultimate authority over all the earth, are clearly foretold in this vital catalogue of prophecies from the great prophet Isaiah.

Isaiah 53: The Greatest Messianic Passage

None of the passages we have considered, however, matches one section from the Book of Isaiah. It is Isaiah 52:13 to 53:12, the greatest of all the prophecies in the Old Testament to the suffering, rejection and ultimate glory of the coming Messiah. It is written in, what radio operators would describe in wartime, *plain language*. In crucial situations radio messages would be sent directly in straightforward terms. Normally some form of coding would be used but, in vital cases, the message would be sent without consideration for security or its origin. A good example is the occasion when British naval aircraft unwittingly attacked HMS Sheffield in the Atlantic Ocean, thinking it was the Bismarck. An immediate command to call off the attack was sent in "plain language," meaning the cessation of the attack was more important than the enemy's ability to discover what was happening.

Isaiah 53 is written in such language. No allegories, symbols or other language requiring interpretation is used. The enemy can have no doubt as to what is being conveyed. Deliberate, unambiguous and straightforward language is used that defies interpretation. It is the most remarkable testimony, seven hundred years before the event, of the event of the crucifixion of the Christ *and* its atoning purpose. Remembering that it is part of a Jewish Scripture, belonging to a people who deny that Jesus is the Messiah, yet it confirms the death, atoning purpose, and resurrection of the great Deliverer to come. It is therefore an *independent* witness to our Gospel, from a source traditionally hostile to it, yet written in such forthright language, that its meaning and implications cannot be missed by anyone open to the truth. Let's go through it as you might if sitting with Muslims who are giving you an opportunity to state your case.

It contains typical Messianic terminology, such as we have already considered. It begins "Behold, my servant shall prosper, he shall be exalted and lifted up, and shall be very high" (Isaiah 52:13). The prophecy begins by predicting the eventual glory of the Messiah. Yet it suddenly changes its emphasis and projects him, firstly, as a suffering servant with no comeliness to recommend him:

> As many were astonished at him! His appearance was so marred, beyond human semblance, and his form beyond that of the sons of men. *Isaiah 52:14*

Having introduced him in anonymity and apparent failure, it then equally suddenly announces his ultimate triumph over all the nations of the earth, such as has never been witnessed before:

> So shall he startle many nations; kings shall shut their mouths because of him; for that which has not been told them they shall see, and that which they have not heard they shall understand. *Isaiah 52:15*

Isaiah was astonished and somewhat bewildered at what he was seeing. Israel had long awaited its promised Messiah since he was promised to David as one of his offspring, yet here, although glory is to come, Isaiah sees that he will first appear almost in obscurity and be rejected as an impostor no different to many who had gone before him. So he asks "Who has believed what we have heard? And to whom has the arm of the Lord been revealed?" (Isaiah 53:1). He recognises that it will take a special revelation from the Lord for anyone to recognise that, at his first coming, this is indeed God's glorious Messiah. For he will appear to be an outcast, a stranger, one from whom men instinctively turn away. He would be neither handsome, rich nor imposing:

> He had no form of comeliness that we should look at him, and no beauty that we should desire him. *Isaiah 53:2*

In hindsight it is easy to comprehend the next passage, knowing that Jesus was apprehended, spat upon, cursed and disowned; yet in Isaiah's time, and at any other time, a suffering saviour would have been unheard of in Israel, a subject for ridicule and scorn. Yet as he foresees the status of God's Messiah during his first advent, Isaiah declares:

> He was despised and rejected by men, a man of sorrows, and acquainted with grief; and as one from whom men hide their faces. He was despised, and we esteemed him not.
>
> *Isaiah 53:3*

As we have said, the prophet is speaking plainly and not in any figures of speech. It is as direct and intense a vision of the reception of Jesus, God's eternal Saviour, as you could wish for. Yet the prophet is immediately given an understanding of why God's Deliverer should be so treated. He sees, in the clearest terms possible, that *this was done for our sins and iniquities that we might be redeemed*, He recognises that the Saviour must first become like us in our degradation before we can become like him in his eternal glory. So he expresses this atoning purpose emphatically:

> Surely he has borne our griefs and carried our sorrows; yet we esteemed him stricken, smitten by God, and afflicted. But *he* was wounded for *our* transgressions, *he* was bruised for *our* iniquities; upon *him* was the chastisement that makes *us* whole, and with *his* stripes *we* are healed. *Isaiah 53:4*

I have deliberately emphasised the pronouns in italics to bring home the essential thrust of the prophet's message: *he will suffer in our place*. Seven centuries before Jesus came into the world one of the great prophets of Israel saw it all. He was coming to be God's Saviour by taking on himself the punishment that is due to us all. The next verse puts it in a nutshell, and you will do well to remind your Muslim hearers that you are quoting from a Jewish scripture and not a book of Christian propaganda:

> All we like sheep have gone astray; we have turned every one to his own way; and the Lord has laid on him the iniquity of us all. *Isaiah 53:6*

This is fundamental Christian language, yet is written in the scripture of a nation that denies that Jesus is the Saviour of the world just as emphatically as Islam does. In the plainest possible language you have here a testimony to the atoning work of the Christ. The passage continues. He was oppressed and afflicted, yet he did not open his mouth to speak in his defence or avoid the false charges against him. This is just what Jesus did. "Like a lamb that is led to the slaughter, and like a sheep that before its shearers is dumb, so he opened not his mouth" (Isaiah 53:7). You can quote the incident in the New Testament where the Apostle Philip met an Ethiopian prince on the way back home who was reading this very passage of scripture. When the Ethiopian asked Philip of whom the prophet spoke, he *told him the good news of Jesus* (Acts 8:35). The New Testament confirms that Jesus was silent in answer to the false charges brought against him that led to his crucifixion (Matthew 26:63, John 19:9). Isaiah marvelled at what he was seeing. Who would imagine that God's glorious Messiah, the supremely anointed one of Israel, greater than Abraham, Moses and David, would be cut off ignominiously from the land of the living, stricken for the transgressions of his people? (v.8). Then comes another riddle similar to the one we considered in the chapter on the Psalms of David (Psalm 22:18 read with John 19:24):

> And they made his grave with the wicked and with a rich man in his death. *Isaiah 53:9*

Once again we have synonyms mixed with antonyms, in contrast to the usual Hebrew style of repeating a statement for emphasis with two synonyms. Grave and death are the synonyms, wicked and rich are the antonyms. Following the usual style of Hebrew poetry the writer might have said his grave was made with the wicked, in his death he was buried with the despised and rejected. Yet it says the opposite. He would be given the dignity of a rich man's burial. No one, prior to the coming of Jesus, could have possibly explained this riddle. The crucifixion narrative, centuries later, gives the explanation:

> When it was evening, there came a rich man from Arimathea, named Joseph, who was also a disciple of Jesus. He went to Pilate and asked for the body of Jesus. Then Pilate ordered it to be given to him. And Joseph took the body, and laid it in a clean linen shroud, and laid it in his own new tomb, which he had hewn in the rock. *Matthew 27:57-60*

Like any other criminal condemned to death, his body would normally have been thrown into the pit of Gehenna, but the intervention of Joseph of Arimathea ensured he was buried with full dignity in an honourable tomb. Once again, as in Psalm 22, you can show Muslims that details of the crucifixion of Jesus were spelled out in the finest possible detail, even in apparent riddles, centuries before the event of his crucifixion came to pass. Yet it is not only the crucifixion and atoning work of Jesus that are here predicted. His resurrection is too, as we see in the next verse:

> When he makes himself an offering for sin, he shall see his offspring, he shall prolong his days; the will of the Lord shall prosper in his hand; he shall see the fruit of the travail of his soul and be satisfied. *Isaiah 53:11*

His atoning work is then again emphasised: God's servant will make many to be accounted righteous; and he shall bear their iniquities (v.11). The Apostle Paul is the great apostle of the atoning work of Jesus by which he saves us from our sins and makes it possible for his righteousness to be imputed to us. It is the fundamental theme of his Epistle to the Romans. Yet here, centuries earlier, we find one of the great prophets of God saying the very same thing. This great, archetypical prophecy of the crucifixion, saving work and resurrection of Jesus, in the clearest possible language, concludes with these words:

> He poured out his soul to death, and was numbered with the transgressors; yet he bore the sin of many, and made intercession with the transgressors. *Isaiah 53:12*

Once again Isaiah emphasises the essence of what he is foretelling: God's Saviour would die, be put to death with other criminals as if he were one of them (Jesus was crucified between two thieves), yet he would intercede for them all. He prayed for the forgiveness of his executioners (Luke 23:34) as well as promising one of his fellow sufferers that he would be with him in Paradise that very day (Luke 23:43). Jesus himself also said, on the very night when this whole prophecy would be fulfilled:

> For I tell you that this scripture must be fulfilled in me, "And he was reckoned with the transgressors," for what is written about me has its fulfilment. *Luke 22:37*

You will find no other passage in the Old Testament where the whole Christian Gospel is foretold in such conspicuous detail, and without any possible ambiguity, as this one. It will also be useful to inform your Muslim hearers that, amongst the so-called Dead Sea Scrolls found at Qumran in 1948, were two almost complete manuscripts of the prophecy of Isaiah, both containing this passage (Isaiah 52:13 - 53:12) in perfect detail, written by hand at least a hundred years before Jesus was crucified. So we have tangible, hand-written evidence that this prophecy predates the unique events it describes in such graphic detail.

The Bible says that thc Word of God is living and active, sharper than any two-edged sword, and you should use it freely in witnessing to Muslims. You do not need to give too much emphasis to the implications of passages such as this one. By simply going through them you will be able to impress the truth on Muslims as the Spirit of God empowers his Word to bring non-believers to the saving knowledge of our Lord Jesus Christ.

There could not be a better place to bring our study of the Old Testament prophecies of the glory of Jesus to a close. We proceed to the New Testament and the greatest of all prophetic messengers, God's own Son, Jesus Christ himself.

Part Two:

The New Testament

Lord and Saviour

Jesus

Unique in the Qur'an and the Bible

Common Features in the Two Books

We have come to the New Testament and, obviously, Jesus Christ himself immediately becomes the key figure. All the Old Testament prophetic narratives that we have considered point to him, now we will consider the Christian Saviour himself and how you can use common ground between the Qur'an and the Bible to witness to Muslims of his salvation and glory. We will begin with the unique features we find in both books, where they are in complete agreement, and see how you can use them to share the Gospel in all its fullness.

1. The Virgin-Birth of Jesus

The Bible records the unique conception of Jesus by a virgin woman, Mary, as a fulfilment of a prophecy seven centuries earlier that such an event would occur and that the son to be born would be known as Immanuel, namely "God with us" (Isaiah 7:14). The annunciation to Mary is recorded in these words:

> In the sixth month the Angel Gabriel was sent from God to a city of Galilee named Nazareth, to a virgin betrothed to a man whose name was Joseph, of the house of David; and the virgin's name was Mary. And he came to her and said "Hail, O favoured one, the Lord is with you." But she was greatly troubled at the saying and considered in her mind what sort of greeting this might be. And the angel said to her "Do not be afraid, Mary, for you have found favour with God. And behold, you will conceive in your womb and bear a son, and you shall call his name Jesus." *Luke 1:26-31*

When Mary replied "How shall this be, since I have no husband?" (v.34), the angel explained that the Holy Spirit would come upon her and that the power of the Most High would overshadow her, giving her the miracle of a virgin-birth. Matthew's Gospel also covers this subject, though here it is Joseph's role that is focused on after Mary had already become pregnant. When he thought she had been unfaithful to him and resolved to put her away quietly, the Angel Gabriel also appeared to him and confirmed that she had conceived by the power of the Holy Spirit (Matthew 1:18-21).

The Qur'an also records the vision to Mary and the virgin-birth of Jesus in two passages. The first reads as follows:

> When the angels said "O Mary! Allah announces to you a Word from himself, whose name is the Messiah, Jesus, son of Mary, and to be honoured in this world and the hereafter, and of those who draw near. He will speak to the people in his infancy and in maturity, and will be one of the righteous." She said "How shall I bear a son when no one has touched me?" He replied "Even so, Allah creates what he wills. When he decrees a matter, he only says to it Be! and it comes to be." *Surah 3:45-47*

In the second passage the annunciation is dealt with in more detail and Mary is promised that her son will be a revelation for mankind and a mercy from Allah (Surah 19:16-22). If one had to ask why Jesus should be born in such a unique way, as no other human being has ever been so conceived, the Qur'an gives a clear answer. She was to conceive Jesus in a *special* way because there was to be something *unique and special about her son.* The virgin-birth is given constant emphasis in the Muslim scripture in the title it gives consistently to Jesus, namely *ibn Maryam*, the son of Mary. No other woman is named in the Qur'an.

2. The Sinlessness of Jesus

According to the Bible Jesus is the only person who ever lived who was entirely without sin. The book charges all men, from Adam onwards, as being under the power of sin (Romans 3:9) and as having sinned and fallen short of the glory of God (Romans 3:23). Only Jesus is excepted. A typical passage declaring his absolute integrity reads:

> He committed no sin, no guile was found on his lips.
> *1 Peter 2:22*

Other passages confirm this. God made him to be sin, *who knew no sin*, so that we might become the righteousness of God in him (2 Corinthians 5.21). We know that Jesus appeared to take away sins, and *in him there is no sin* (1 John 3:5). The Qur'an, too, declares that Jesus was without sin. When the Angel Jibril (Gabriel) appeared to Mary to announce her conception of Jesus, he said:

> I am only a messenger of your Lord, to announce to you a faultless son. *Surah 19:19*

The words used in Arabic to describe him are *ghulaaman-zakiyyan*, "a most-holy boy." The word *zakiyya*, meaning "blameless," appears only twice in the Qur'an. The other occasion is in a story about Moses in which he was on a journey with an unnamed companion who had been sent to guide him into deeper knowledge and understanding. At length they met a young man and his companion, known in Islam as *al-Khidr*, "the Green One," a mysterious figure who is said to appear to holy men from time to time, immediately slew him without giving any reason for doing so. Moses asked why he had slain an innocent person who had not slain anyone else? The companion ordered him to be patient, to which Moses responded that he should not have questioned him.

The word for "innocent," in this context again meaning blameless, is *zakiyya*. Moses was only referring to the young man's innocence of any crime deserving death, but in Jesus' case the angel was describing his whole personality and character before he was even born. "Faultless," or blameless, clearly means *without sin*. So the Qur'an confirms the Biblical teaching that Jesus was the only sinless person who would ever live as the Qur'an nowhere describes anyone else in this way. On the contrary the Qur'an acknowledges the sins of the other prophets and specifically refers to the sins of Adam (Surah 7:23), Abraham (26:82), Moses (28:16), Jonah (37:142) and Muhammad (47:19, 48:2). In the case of Muhammad the Qur'an expressly commands him to ask forgiveness (*wastaghfir*) of his sins (*dhanbika*). The words used are employed throughout the Qur'an in the same context and there can be no doubt about their meaning, despite the subtle attempts of many Muslim commentators to reduce them to less imposing terms (such as to ask for "protection" from his "shortcomings").

3. The Ascension of Jesus to Heaven

The New Testament teaches, again and again, that after his resurrection from the dead, Jesus ascended to heaven in bodily form. The narrative recording this event reads as follows:

> And when he had said this, as they were looking on, he was lifted up, and a cloud took him out of their sight. And while they were

> gazing into heaven as he went, behold, two men stood by in white robes, and said, "Men of Galilee, why do you stand looking into heaven? This Jesus, who was taken up from you into heaven, will come in the same way as you saw him go into heaven."
>
> *Acts 1:9-11*

In other passages the New Testament teaches that Jesus is seated at the right hand of God (Colossians 3:1), that God made him sit at his right hand in the heavenly places, far above all rule, authority, power and dominion (Ephesians 1:21) and that he taught that he was to return to heaven whence he had originally come (John 6:62, 16:28). The Qur'an only has one statement to confirm the ascension of Jesus but it has been enough to convince Muslims throughout the world that he is there to this day, alive in the very presence of Allah. The text reads:

> But Allah took him up to himself. *Surah 4:158*

This statement is made in contrast to the claim of the Jews that they had killed the Messiah, Jesus, the son of Mary, and Muslims believe he was rescued from crucifixion and taken to heaven without dying. Despite the different circumstances, both the Qur'an and the Bible teach the ascension of Jesus, alive and in bodily form, from earth to heaven. Significantly the only Hadith records mentioning the destiny of Jesus agree without exception that Jesus was taken to heaven.

4. The Second Coming of Jesus

The last significant feature about Jesus, where the Qur'an and the Bible are in agreement, is his return to the earth from heaven at the end of time. It is one of the grandest and most extensive subject of the prophetic texts of the New Testament as the following quotes show:

> Then will appear the sign of the Son of man in heaven, and then all the tribes of the earth will mourn, and they will see the Son of man coming on the clouds of heaven with power and great glory.
>
> *Matthew 24:30*

> For the Lord himself will descend from heaven with a cry of command, with the archangel's call, and with the sound of the trumpet of God. *1 Thessalonians 4:16*

> Behold he is coming with the clouds, and every eye will see him, every one who pierced him; and all tribes of the earth will wail on account of him. *Revelation 1:7*

According to the Bible Jesus will return from heaven at the end of time in his glory, with all his holy angels with him, and will bring in the Day of Judgment. All the nations will be gathered before him and he will separate them, to glory or destruction, as a shepherd separates the sheep from the goats (Matthew 25:32). The Qur'an, once again, only deals with this subject in one verse but it has led to a consensus throughout the Muslim world that Jesus will one day return from heaven to earth. The text reads:

> And he shall be a sign for the hour. *Surah 43:61*

The verse can be literally translated "And there is knowledge (*ilm*) of the hour (*saah*)" and it can be argued that the return of Jesus is rather arbitrarily read into the text, yet many of the companions of Muhammad in his lifetime confirmed that he taught that there is a specific allusion to the return of Jesus shortly before the hour of judgment in this verse, including Ibn Abbas, Hasan and Qatawa. Many Hadith records confirm the return of Jesus, one of which teaches that he will institute a reign of peace (*Sahih Muslim, Vol.1, p.93*). Another teaches that Jesus will return to receive the homage of all the peoples, Jews, Christians and Muslims, in fulfilment of Surah 4:159 (*Sahih al-Bukhari, Vol.4, p.137*).

Yet another teaches that he is alive in heaven, will return as a ruler of the whole earth, and will then die like all other living beings (*Ibn Sa'd, Kitab al-Tabaqat al-Kabir, Vol.1, p.47*). Muslims generally believe that he will land on a minaret of the great mosque in Damascus, that he will lead the whole world to follow Islam, will die after forty years, and will be buried next to Muhammad in his grave in Medina. There are once again differences between Christianity and Islam in their interpretations of what will happen when Jesus returns, but both believe in the second coming and base that belief on the teachings of the Bible and the Qur'an respectively.

Implications of the Uniqueness of Jesus

We have outlined four features in the life of Jesus which are taught in both books. What can we learn from them and can Christians find effective points of witness here to Muslims? I personally believe that, as the chapters on Abraham and Isaac earlier in this book give the best grounds for witness from the Old Testament, so this one gives the best foundation from the New Testament. These four features show, firstly, that Jesus was *quite unique* in the history of mankind and, secondly, that this uniqueness implies *singular greatness* such as no other prophet or figurehead has ever possessed. Let us look firstly at the uniqueness of Jesus in each feature and, as we proceed, at the key sources of his greatness.

The **virgin-birth** of Jesus was unique. No one else was ever born without a father. What, we need to ask, was the *reason* for this exceptional birth? God, surely, does not do unusual things arbitrarily if they are unnecessary. Something must have required that Jesus be born in this way. To put it simply, there must have been something *unique* about Jesus himself. In both the Bible and the Qur'an Mary is described as the greatest among women:

> Blessed are you among women, and blessed is the fruit of your womb. *Luke 1:42*

> And when the angels said, O Mary! Surely Allah has chosen you and purified you, and preferred you above the women of the world. *Surah 3:42*

Why is Mary exalted in these passages above all other women? It is because she was the mother of *Jesus*, because she mothered *the greatest among men*. There was something unique about her son that made it necessary for him to be born of a virgin woman. The reason was given by Jesus himself. He was not an ordinary man born in the normal course of procreation. He taught that he had existed in the heavens before the foundation of the universe and had witnessed the fall of Satan (Luke 10.18). He also taught that he had come down from heaven (John 6.38), that he would ascend where he was before (John 6.62), and that he came from the Father into the world and would leave the world and return to the Father (John 16.28).

This is why he was born of a virgin woman. He *pre-existed* his earthly life and had come into the world *from heaven* and had assumed human form. He had, therefore a unique beginning to his life just as it would end in a unique way. He came from heaven and would return there. Jesus himself drew a sharp contrast between himself and all other men when he said to the Jews "You are from below, I am from above. You are of this world, I am not of this world" (John 8:23). Here you can show Muslims that Jesus is different from, and indeed superior to, all the prophets who went before him. In what way, however, was he greater than all other men? The Angel Gabriel gave the answer when he said to Mary:

> He will be great and will be called the Son of the Most High ... therefore the child to be born will be called holy, the Son of God. *Luke 1:32,35*

Adam was created from dust and all other men, prophets and patriarchs included, have been made from the same dust. Jesus, however, was conceived solely by the Spirit of God because he is the Son of God. Here you can show Muslims very emphatically why Jesus had to be born of a virgin woman. Muslims can give no other answer to his unique birth than to say it was by the power and the word of God (Surah 3:59). They cannot explain the reasons why Jesus, and particularly Jesus, alone should be born so uniquely. It could hardly have been no more than a manifestation of God's power for it would have required a very limited exercise of that power and could not have been physically proved. It was a very unique event and must have had a unique cause.

That cause is the fact that Jesus is the eternal Son of God, who pre-existed all men, who became the Son of man, the man Christ Jesus.

He was also unique in his **sinlessness**. Not only does the Bible regard all other human beings who have ever existed as sinners, implicated in the sin of the first man Adam, but the Hadith records also state that Muhammad regarded all human beings as sinners other than Jesus. In the first chapter we met his statement "Every son of Adam is a sinner" (*Sunan Ibn Majah, Vol.5, p.489*) and here is another to the same effect:

> Abu Huraira reported Allah's Messanger (saw) as saying: The satan touches every son of Adam on the day when his mother gives birth to him with the exception of Mary and her son.
>
> *Sahih Muslim, Vol.4, p.1261*

Why would Jesus alone be sinless among men? Again the Muslim world can give no reason for this. Muslims may respond by saying to you that all prophets had some unique features, but in the case of Jesus we find that his uniqueness is *personal to himself*, that is, that he himself is unique in his birth, sinlessness, ascension and second coming. There is no comparison here with any other prophet. All of these unique features, spanning the origin of his life, its conclusion and final destiny, are found in him alone. You need to impress Muslims with these unique distinctions. In this verse we find the cause of Jesus' unique sinlessness:

> Jesus said to them, "Truly, truly, I say to you, the Son can do nothing of his own accord, but only what he sees the Father doing; for whatever he does, that the Son does likewise."
>
> *John 5:19*

It is because Jesus is the *Son of God* that he is sinless. He taught that he and the Father are one (John 10:30) and he will, therefore, always do the will of his Father. If he did anything independently of the Father, he would no longer be one with him. One who is always doing the absolute will of his Father cannot sin against him. This is why he is sinless - because, as the Son of God, he too is absolutely holy and always does what is pleasing to the Father (John 8:29).

The third point of uniqueness is his **ascension to heaven**. The reason for this is implied in his virgin-birth and the texts we have already quoted. He ascended to heaven because *he came from there in the first place*. If he had returned to dust as all other men do, no Christian would believe that he was the unique Son of God. You can point out to Muslims that these unique features not only, with one accord, support his teaching that he is the Son of God, but that they are essential features if this teaching is to be proved true. If he is the Son of God he must be born uniquely of a virgin to become man. He must be sinless and he cannot return to the dust. He must return to his Father in heaven. Conversely, if he is not the Son of God as the Qur'an teaches, these unique features have no meaning or relevance. By conceding them the Qur'an is unwittingly confirming Christian belief.

The Qur'an often speaks of the throne of God (Surahs 10:4, 7:54, 13:2 etc). This expresses the royal sovereignty which God enjoys over the whole universe. The Bible makes the same point but, to emphasise the unique ascension of Jesus to heaven and his ultimate place there, it declares that he sat down at his right hand as sons of kings in those days sat at their father's side, being the heirs to the throne. Many passages make this clear, such as the following two:

> God accomplished his great might in Christ when he raised him from the dead and made him sit at his right hand in the heavenly places. *Ephesians 1:20*

> Now the point in what we are saying is this: we have such a high priest, one who is seated at the right hand of the throne of the Majesty in heaven. *Hebrews 8:1*

When Stephen saw the heavens opened just before his martyrdom, he declared that he saw the Son of man standing at the right hand of God (Acts 7:56). Jesus also declared that he would grant to all who conquer the right to sit at his right hand, just as he had conquered and sat down with his Father on his throne (Revelation 3:21). The Qur'an speaks of the throne of

God - the rightful place of Jesus after his ascension to heaven is at the right hand of him who sits upon it.

Lastly, let us look at the uniqueness of the fourth feature, the **return of Jesus to earth**. Though he has been in heaven for almost two thousand years already, no Christian or Muslim expects him to return looking like an old man. He will return looking not a day older than when he left. Why will Jesus return to earth? As we have seen, Muslims expect him to establish a universal rule, become a follower of Muhammad, and be buried next to him after his death. You can well ask Muslims why Jesus should return to earth only to die and be buried. It makes no sense.

Jesus will return for a far greater reason. We need again to ask why there should be this unique feature in his life and why it is Jesus who will fulfil it. It is because he is the Son of God and, having died on the cross for sinners, will bring both the salvation and judgment of God at the end of time. By becoming man the Son of God has also become the obvious medium of the judgment of God. Firstly, he revealed God to men. The Qur'an only professes to reveal the will and attributes of God. Jesus revealed God himself to men as this passage shows:

> All things have been delivered to me by my Father; and no one knows the Son except the Father, and no one knows the Father except the Son and anyone to whom the Son chooses to reveal him.
>
> *Matthew 11:27*

Elsewhere Jesus taught that he who sees him sees the Father who sent him (John 12:45, 14:9) and that there was no way to the Father but by him (John 14:6). Being the Son of God in human form, he reveals the fulness of God to men. Once having lived on earth, *no one can identify now with God other than through him.* This is the second reason why he is the medium of the judgment of God. He has brought men face-to-face with God. This comes out very clearly in another statement he made:

> For as the Father has life in himself, so he has granted the Son to have life in himself also, and has given him authority to execute judgment, because he is the Son of man.
>
> *John 5:26-27*

This alone explains why Jesus will return to earth. He comes to save those who have been redeemed through his blood, and he comes to judge the rest. Thus the second coming harmonises with the uniqueness of Jesus as the Son of God.

In the four unique features of Jesus' life you have tremendous evidence to witness to Muslims of who he is and why he came into the world and will return. What is fascinating, and supports your witness, is that the Qur'an and Hadith support these features and acknowledge them all! Despite denying the deity of Jesus, by admitting these features it is tacitly and unreservedly implying that he is indeed the Son of God. Even though he lived as a man on earth, everything we know about him ultimately places him on the level of deity more than that of humanity.

The Son of God

The Messiah, Spirit and Word

The Qur'anic Rejection of the Deity of Jesus

We have looked at some of the unique features in the life of Jesus that distinguish him from all the other prophets of God and which, when considered together, show that he is far greater than all of them and is, indeed, the Son of God. We will now turn to three titles of Jesus which are found in both the Qur'an and the Bible and see how these, too, can be used in leading Muslims to the fulness of Christ. We will be considering only one text from the Qur'an simply because all three titles appear in it and in a most interesting context. In fact, from a Christian point of view, this text is pivotal when assessing just who Jesus really is in Islam, for it shows a strong contrast, even a complete contradiction, between the Muslim dogma that Jesus is not the Son of God and the implications of this text that he most certainly is! The text is:

> O People of the Scripture! Do not exaggerate in your religion and do not say anything of Allah than the truth. Verily the Messiah, Jesus son of Mary, is only a messenger of Allah, and his Word which he bestowed on Mary, and a Spirit from him. So believe in Allah and his messengers. And do not say "Three"! Desist, it is better. Verily Allah is only One. Glorified be he, than that he should ever have a son. To him is everything in the heavens and on the earth. And sufficient is Allah as an overseer. Surah 4:171

There is a threefold denial of the deity of Jesus in this verse. Firstly, Christians are commanded not to believe in Jesus as one of three gods (an allusion to the Trinity). Allah is only one God, thus Jesus cannot be another. Finally, the glory of Allah is too great for him to ever have a Son. (The Qur'an, on the few occasions it refers to the Trinity in whatever form

Muhammad comprehended it, denounces it as a combination of Jesus and his mother Mary as two gods alongside Allah - cf. Surah 5:76-78, 5:110).

Other passages of the Qur'an reject the deity of Jesus and the Christian belief in him as the Son of God equally emphatically (Surahs 9:30, 19:35), but the text quoted has perhaps the most comprehensive denial of all. What more can you want than a threefold repudiation? Yet, as we shall see, when you consider the titles of Jesus in the same verse, you find a threefold *confirmation* that Jesus is indeed the eternal Son of God.

Debating the subject purely as an either\or - he was or he wasn't the Son of God - rarely leads to anything more than further polarisation between Christians and Muslims as they fall back on their predetermined dogmatics. Yet, when you can analyse the meanings of the unique titles given to Jesus in this text, it becomes far easier to witness to Muslims of who Jesus really is and it is this theme that we will be pursuing in this chapter. Once again, from common ground between us, you can witness to the glory of Jesus.

Al-Masih: Jesus the Messiah

In the next chapter we will consider this title in far more detail as it is one of the vital contact points between Christians and Muslims when we consider who Jesus really was, but here we will consider it solely in its context as it appears in Surah 4:171.

Firstly, Jesus alone is called **the Messiah** in the Qur'an. No other prophet, patriarch or priest is given this title. In Arabic it is simply *al-Masih*. The Qur'an makes no attempt to define the title but it does award it to Jesus on no less than eleven occasions. Sometimes it is simply *al-Masih*, "the Messiah" (Surah 5:72), elsewhere it is *al-Masihu Isa*, "the Messiah Jesus" (Surah 4:157), while it also appears as *al-Masihubnu Maryam*, "the Messiah son of Mary" (Surah 5:17). It is a unique title, given to no one else, but applied to Jesus nearly a dozen times.

If you were to ask a Muslim what it means, he really could not tell you other than to say "Jesus is the Messiah." The title actually has no meaning in Islam and is not derived from any Arabic word. It is an arabised form of *ha-Mashiah*, the Hebrew title which does have a meaning, namely "the Anointed One." The Jews had long awaited this coming figurehead, especially after his advent had been announced through all the prophets as we have seen. It was Daniel, however, who first gave the coming Son of David the express title Messiah (Daniel 9:25). Without an explanation in Islam one has to go to the Jewish and Christian scriptures to find its meaning.

Surah 4:171 says Jesus was no more than a messenger but all Jews and Christians know that this specific title, the Messiah, is a man who stands out above all other men, including the other messengers of God. The Old Testament prophecies we have considered and many more show that he would be possessed of a regality, majesty, splendour and excellence above all other men. While denying that Jesus is the Son of God, the Qur'an, nevertheless, is giving him a title that implies that he is the ultimate man of human history and the holy one who was to be the final expression of the revelation of God to men. "God was in the Messiah, reconciling the world to himself" (2 Corinthians 5:19).

The most important issue here, in considering Surah 4:171, is to show Muslims that while the Qur'an denies that Jesus is the Son of God, it is giving him a title that proves unreservedly that he is! In Biblical times the expressions Messiah and Son of God were synonymous. Let us look at some key texts you can quote to Muslims to prove the point.

1. Jewish believers in Jesus

The Jewish disciples of Jesus freely used the two titles, Messiah and Son of God, interchangeably. (Although the Greek texts use the word *Christos*, the Greek word for Messiah meaning "Christ," we will use the original Hebrew designation as it makes the point more forcefully). Simon Peter was one of the first Jewish follower of Jesus to do so:

> You are the Messiah, the Son of the living God.
>
> *Matthew 16:16*

Nathaniel was another who simultaneously called Jesus the Son of God and the King of Israel, another synonym for Messiah (John 1:49). Martha, the sister of Lazarus and Mary, also used the two titles simultaneously in her expression of belief in Jesus:

> I believe you are the Messiah, the Son of God, he who is coming into the world. *John 11:27*

2. Caiaphas, the Jewish High Priest

When Jesus was brought before Caiaphas, the High Priest of Israel, on the night of his trial, Caiaphas also used the titles synonymously when placing Jesus on oath to declare whether he was the Son of God:

> I adjure you, by the living God, tell us if you are the Messiah, the Son of God. *Matthew 26:63*

3. The Early Christian Gospel-Writers

The closest followers of Jesus during his lifetime, and others who followed him shortly after his resurrection and ascension to heaven, also used the titles together in various contexts to declare who Jesus really was. Here are two examples:

> The beginning of the Gospel of Jesus the Messiah, the Son of God. *Mark 1:1*

> These are written that you may believe that Jesus is the Messiah, the Son of God, and that believing you may have life in his name. *John 20:31*

4. Demons who Recognised Him

Even the demons who were chased out of many they had possessed knew that Jesus was both the Messiah and the Son of God. They knew him from all eternity as the eternal Son from the Father and recognised him in human form when he commanded them with authority to depart.

> And demons also came out of many, crying "You are the Son of God!" But he rebuked them, and would not allow them to speak, because they knew that he was the Messiah. *Luke 4:41*

From all these texts we can see how unique the title Messiah is. It is no ordinary title, it is one of the highest eminence and only the Son of God in human form could claim it. This much is obvious from the texts we have quoted. Both the followers of Jesus and his enemies knew who the Messiah really would be.

By admitting that Jesus is the Messiah and by confirming his own emphatic declaration to this effect (John 4:25-26), the Qur'an has duly given Jesus a title which implies that he is the very person that the Qur'an is otherwise at such pains to deny, the Son of God himself. In the next chapter we will see, in more detail, how you can witness to Muslims very effectively on the meaning and outworking of this title.

Kalimatuhu - The Word of God

In the same verse, Surah 4:171, Jesus is also called "His Word." In Surah 3:45 the Qur'an states that the angels, when announcing the unique conception of Jesus to Mary, told her that Allah was giving her good tidings "of a Word from him." The expression here used, in the original Arabic, is *kalimatim-minhu*. Broken up, it means *kalima* (word), *min* (from), *hu* (him). Note this, as we will see this structure again soon. Jesus is the only human being who ever lived who is called **a Word from God**. The same title is applied to him in the Christian Bible:

> He is clad in a robe dipped in blood, and the name by which he is called is the Word of God. *Revelation 19:13*

Once again Jesus is given a title in the Qur'an which the Bible gives him as well. Like the Messiah, this is a very distinctive and remarkable title. It is important to emphasise two specific features of this title in your witness to Muslims. Jesus *himself*, in his actual person, is the Word. Secondly, the source of this Word is *God*. Neither book says that he delivered the word of God as other prophets did, or that he was learned in it, or that he embodied and represented it. He is expressly declared to be a Word *from* God, or the Word *of* God. Other prophets received the messages of God but Jesus, in a unique way, is himself *the* message of God to the world.

As with the title Messiah, the Qur'an attempts no explanation of the title. You may be countered with the suggestion that this is no more than a definition of how Jesus was conceived in the first place when Allah simply said "Be, and he came to be" (Surah 3:47). According to the whole verse, however, this is how anything is created by God. The full text reads "If he decrees a thing, he but says to it Be! and it comes to be." This response is over-simplistic, especially when we read a similar text which says:

> Lo! the likeness of Jesus with Allah is as the likeness of Adam. He created him from dust and said to him: "Be!" and he came to be.
> *Surah 3:59*

So, according to the Qur'an, Jesus was created by the word of God in the same way Adam, and by implication, all men are. The title "His Word" and the similar ascription "a Word from Him" are unique, however. Adam is not called the Word of God in the Qur'an, nor are the angels, nor is any other creature. Jesus alone, as in the Bible, is called the Word of God. The title, in its context, applies to him alone.

There is obviously something about the person of Jesus himself that makes him the Word of God in a way no other man has ever been or ever will be. You need to point out to Muslims that the key to understanding the title is the emphasis of deity as its source. The Word is *from God.* He himself is the communication and revelation of God to men. He does not merely bring the word of God, he is the Word of God. We have to turn to the Bible to find the ultimate meaning of the title in view of the fact that the Qur'an attributes it to Jesus without explanation. We go to the very beginning of John's Gospel where this subject is treated in more detail. It commences with these words:

> In the beginning was the Word. And the Word was with God. And the Word was God. He was in the beginning with God. All things were made through him and without him was not anything made that was made. *John 1:1-2*

When we amplify or paraphrase these words we get a clear picture of the meaning of the title. In the beginning, *before* God ever began to *create*, the Word *already existed.* Far from being part of the created order, the Word was in the realm of God and indeed the very nature of the Word was God. When God first began to fashion the *created* order, the Word already existed in the *divine* order. He himself was not created but all *other* things were created by God *through* him as agent. Because he alone is the Word of God, and is therefore the ultimate means of communication between God and his creatures, nothing was created without being created by and *through* him.

Why is he the Word of God, however? In what way was Jesus uniquely the communication of God in himself to mankind? We go a bit further down the first page of John's Gospel and find these words:

> And the Word became flesh, and dwelt among us, full of grace and truth. *John 1:14*

The title signifies two unique things about the Christian Saviour and distinguish him from all other prophets of God. They are:

1. Every Word of Jesus was the Word of God

All the prophets who went before him spoke the Word of God when moved by the Holy Spirit, but in general conversation their speech was entirely their own. Muslims themselves, believing Muhammad to be the last prophet, distinguish between the Qur'an, which he received and conveyed as the word of God, and his own teachings which are recorded in the Hadith as inspirational but not divine. Jesus, however, *at all times* spoke the word of God, whether in public preaching or in private conversation. He confirmed this on various occasions, as in these two verses:

> I have not spoken on my own authority, but the Father who sent me has given me commandment what to say and what to speak. And I know that his commandment is eternal life. What I say, therefore, I say as the Father has bidden me. *John 12:49-50*

> The words that I say to you I do not speak on my own authority, but the Father who dwells in me does his works.
> *John 14:10*

On other occasions Jesus referred to the word of God which he was proclaiming as his own word. Being the Word of God, there was no distinction. For example, he said that those who do not love him do not keep his words, adding that they were ultimately not his but the Father's who sent him (John 14:24). Other examples are: "He who hears *my word* and believes him who sent me has eternal life" (John 5:24); "If you continue in *my word* you are truly my disciples (John 8:31); and "Yet you have kept *my word* and have not denied my name" (Revelation 3:8).

2. Jesus himself is God's Final Message to Mankind

Being the Word of God, Jesus himself is the final and complete revelation of God to the human race. The following text expresses this perfectly:

> He is the *image* of the invisible God, the first-born of all creation; for *in* him all things were created, in heaven and on earth, visible and invisible, whether thrones or dominions or principalities or authorities - all things were created *through* him and *for* him. He is before all things and in him all things hold together.
> *Colossians 1:15-19*

Jesus himself is the Word of God. There is no independence, therefore, between God and his Word. In human form Jesus embodied the divine being. He was not a created messenger; he is, and for all eternity will be, the eternal Word of God.

Surah 4:171 tells Christians not to exaggerate in their religion and to say nothing of Allah but the truth. Yet, in view of these unique titles we are considering, it is hard to see where the exaggeration is. The text has a threefold denial of the deity of Christ yet, in the titles it applies to him, it simply affirms the very thing it is at such pains to deny! We have already seen that the titles Messiah and Son of God are synonymous. The title Word of God is also interchangeable with the title Son of God. If anything this title is more emphatic and suggestive of deity as it implies no submission on the part of the Word to God as the expression Son to Father does.

The most important thing, however, is to use this title to witness to what it ultimately means in the context of God's message to mankind. The word that we proclaim is the Gospel, the good news of God's saving grace in Jesus Christ. The crucifixion, death and resurrection of Jesus *is* God's message. He died to save us from our sins and rose from the dead to give us an assured hope of one day doing likewise. Instead of being raised to face the judgment, we will be glorified and will share his perfect holiness and righteousness forever. Our sins will not be counted against us. We receive this if we become committed believers in Jesus. This is where you have an open door to witness to Muslims as to why Jesus himself is the Word, God's final message to mankind.

Let us press on to the third title to see how you can communicate the fulness of Jesus to Muslims from this one text in the Qur'an that attempts, more than any other, to avoid it.

Ruhullah - The Spirit of God

In Islam Jesus is given the title *Ruhullah*, meaning "Spirit of God." It comes from the same text, Surah 4:171, where Jesus is called *wa-ruhun-minhu*, "a spirit from him." The same structure is used as for the Word from God: *ruh* (a spirit), *min* (from), *hu* (him). In this case we do find some evidence in the Qur'an that helps us to define the title. The expression occurs again in the following verse:

> These are those in whose hearts he has inscribed faith, and strengthened them with a spirit from himself. *Surah 58:22*

The same words are used as in Surah 4:171, *ruhun-minhu*, "a spirit from him." Nowhere else in the Qur'an does this expression occur. In his commentary on the Qur'an Yusuf Ali says that the "phrase used is stronger" than that for the Holy Spirit (*Ruhul-Quds*) in the Qur'an who is identified in Islam as the Angel Gabriel. He implies that this Spirit from God is greater than the mighty angel identified and says it is "the divine spirit which we can no more define adequately than we can define in human language the nature and attributes of God".

The Muslim commentator has, unintentionally but very impressively, given a precise definition of the Holy Spirit as we known him in the Bible. *He* is the "divine spirit" who cannot be defined in human language with terminology other than that used for God himself. Yet the Qur'an, in the only other place where this expression occurs, applies this same divine title to Jesus. Exactly the same words are used.

So you have a third title in Surah 4:171, Spirit from God, which attributes divine features to Jesus just as the titles Messiah and Word of God do. Significantly they are synonymous with titles used in the Bible for Jesus to further express his profile towards mankind as the eternal Son from the Father. The Qur'an, in the very passage which contains a threefold denial of the deity of Jesus ("Do not say Trinity! God is only one God. Far be it from his glory to have a son") paradoxically attributes three titles to him which affirm the very same thing! He is the Anointed Son of God, the Messiah; he is the divine Word of God, and he is a Spirit coming from God. Jesus was not just another prophet called to office at an appropriate point in time. He is the message of God, he came from God, his very spirit is the Spirit of God.

You have remarkable material here for a positive witness to Muslims of the fact that Jesus is the Son of God and God's divine messenger, his last word, to the human race. Uniquely, however, you can take this last title further with Muslims. The Qur'an, in its use of the expression *ruhun-minhu* that the Qur'an unwittingly affirms the Trinity!

Yusuf Ali freely concedes that this is no created spirit of which the books teaches but the *divine* spirit, which comes from God, and must be defined in the same terms as God. Twice the Qur'an uses the expression, once for Jesus Christ, and once for the Spirit which comes from God and strengthens believers. A closer definition of the Trinity you could hardly hope to find. Surah 58:22 defines the Spirit from God in terms synonymous with those applied to the Holy Spirit in the Bible while Surah 4:171 expressly nominates Jesus in the same terms.

As with the title Word of God, you have here a golden opportunity for witness. God is spirit, Jesus taught, and those who worship him must worship in spirit and in truth (John 4:24). The trouble with all men and women is that sin has deadened the spirit in us and a rebirth is necessary to come into a living relationship with God. Islam is, in practice, primarily a religion of forms and rituals. Not only are the five times of daily prayers prescribed but so is every detail of the prior ablutions and, thereafter, the performance of the *salaat*. The Hajj Pilgrimage is also prescribed down to the last detail. Once a man turns to God and believes in Jesus, the Spirit of God enters into him and unites him to God. He is now strengthened by the power of God's Spirit to become the person God really wants him to be. He enters into a living relationship with God and comes to know him personally. This is certainly what the Bible teaches when it reveals that Jesus was a spirit from God, sent to redeem us, and that the Holy Spirit from God enters into our hearts to make us become the living children of God.,

In the titles which the Qur'an gives to Jesus, especially those we have considered in Surah 4:171 which are synonymous with similar titles given to Jesus in the New Testament, you have common ground with Muslims and a wonderful opportunity to witness to them of who he really is - God's anointed deliverer, his own Word, and a spirit proceeding directly from his own being.

Let us look at the title *al-Masih* in greater detail as there is much more material here for witness to his uniqueness and unparalleled saving grace.

Al-Masihu Isa

God's Anointed Messiah

Ha Mashiah: The Hope of Israel

For centuries, from the time of the great prophetic period, when Isaiah, Jeremiah, Ezekiel and a host of other prophets had foretold the final purposes of God for the Israelite nation and the world as a whole, to the time of the Roman occupation, Israel had longed for its promised Messiah, the Son of David, who they believed would redeem them from all their troubles. The nation longed for its Deliverer and, knowing from prophecies we have already considered in this book, that he would be descended from their great king David, named him the Son of David. Yet they chose a more popular title to readily define him, namely the Messiah. By the time of Pontius Pilate, Herod Antipas, and the high priests Annas and Caiaphas, Messianic fervour among the Israelites was at fever pitch. His advent seemed overdue as they yearned for a glorious king who would establish their nation as the dominant nation over the whole earth.

The title Messiah comes from the Hebrew *ha Mashiah*, meaning "the Anointed One." *Mashiah* is a common Hebrew word and, in the Hebrew Old Testament, is applied to the anointed high priest (Leviticus 4:3), the nation's king (2 Samuel 1:14), the prophets of God (Psalm 105:15) and even the Persian king Cyrus (Isaiah 45:1). All of these were anointed by God for some specific ministry or purpose, yet, from the abundance of prophecies of a supreme deliverer to come, who is called *mashiah* in Daniel 9:25, the people of Israel determined that a supremely anointed figure would arise whom they named *the* Messiah.

Because the Qur'an acknowledges this title (*al-Masih*) and applies it exclusively to Jesus Christ eleven times, this subject is a valid and crucial one for Christian witness to Muslims. The Qur'an, as a rule, teaches that all the prophets of God were the same and that Jesus was no more than a prophet, yet here we have a title obviously derived from its Hebrew equivalent, which to the Israelite nation implied so much more. Prophets had come and gone yet one supreme ruler, who would overshadow them all, had been promised in their prophetic writings and they longed for his coming.

The New Testament confirms that Jesus was indeed the Messiah and, while it generally uses the Greek title *ho Christos* ("the Christ") to describe him, it does on two occasions confirm that this is a translation of the word *Messias*, the Greek word for Messiah (John 1:41, 4:25). Once again, therefore, we find common ground with Muslims and you have a solid foundation from which to witness to the saving grace of our Saviour Jesus Christ and just what the title Messiah means. In the chapter on the prophecies of Isaiah I quoted a number of prophetic texts you can use in witness on this subject but a few others from other Old Testament prophets are useful here as well. Here is one from the prophecy of Zechariah:

> Behold the man whose name is the Branch; for he shall grow up in his place, and he shall build the temple of the Lord. It is he who shall build the temple of the Lord, and shall bear royal honour, and shall sit and rule upon his throne. *Zechariah 6:12-13*

It was texts like these that made the Jews expect a glorious king who would rule over the world from Jerusalem but, as we saw in the chapter on Isaiah, prophecies of his regal glory were interwoven with prophecies of suffering, obscurity and humiliation. The Jews failed to realise that he would come in humility the first time as a suffering servant to become exactly like us and, through his death on the cross, deliver us from our sins. Only at his second coming would he come as the divine ruler of the universe to establish his eternal kingdom and raise his followers to glory, to become as he is in his perfect righteousness. The Jews thought he would deliver the nation from the Romans. Jesus, God's Messiah, came to deliver all of us from ourselves, and from the powers of the world, the flesh and the devil, to pull us down into a state of hostility with God.

It is important, in witnessing to Muslims on the title *al-Masih*, to show that all the promises made by the earlier prophets had this twofold emphasis, a suffering servant and a glorious king. The people of Israel seem to have conveniently overlooked the first, yet Muslims recognise that Jesus will have two lifetimes on earth, the first when he was God's servant, born of Mary, and the second when he will return as a ruler of all the earth for forty years. Many Christians also hold the view that Jesus will return to reign over the earth, expecting him to govern it from Jerusalem for a period of a thousand years. In my view both the Muslims and Christians who hold this belief are making the same mistake the Jews made - expecting an earthly king who would rule from an earthly throne. The Bible makes it plain he will usher in an eternal kingdom and that he will rule directly from his Father's throne in heaven (Revelation 3:21). You need to draw this contrast, otherwise the Messiah of God looks like nothing more than another king David.

The Messiah: Greater Than All the prophets

In witness to Muslims on the identity of the Messiah, this point is crucial before you go into the greater work he was called to perform. He was not just another prophet in a long line of earthly messengers, he was the eternal Saviour, the anointed Messiah, who came down from heaven to reconcile men to God.

John the Baptist is regarded as a prophet in Islam, *Yahya alayhis-salaam* (John on whom be peace), just like all the other prophets. What is unique about him is that he lived at the same time as Jesus and was able to witness directly to him. This is what he said of him in his Messianic vocation:

> You yourselves bear me witness that I said "I am not the Messiah but I have been sent before him" ... he must increase but I must decrease. *John 3:28,30*

> This is he of whom I said, "After me comes a man who ranks before me, for he was before me." *John 1:30*

John clearly regarded the Messiah as a representative of God far greater than himself, and in this he was only emulating all the prophets who went before him. As Jesus said, Abraham rejoiced to see his day (John 8:56), Moses foresaw his coming (John 5:46), and David called him his Lord (Matthew 22:45). John the Baptist knew that he had only been sent as a forerunner of the Messiah. As the New Testament says, "he was not the light, but came to bear witness to the light" (John 1:8). Jesus is the light of the world, as he himself said (John 8:12), and everything that was written of him in the law of Moses, the psalms of David, and the writings of the other prophets, had to be fulfilled (Luke 24:44). the Samaritan woman who met Jesus at Jacob's well near Sychar in Samaria also knew the Messiah would be far greater than all the prophets who preceded him. She said to Jesus:

> I know the Messiah is coming, he who is called Christ; when he comes, he will show us all things. *John 4:25*

To this statement Jesus openly replied "I who speak to you am he" (John 4:26). You can show Muslims that this question was a direct invitation to Jesus to disclose his true identity - was he just another prophet or was he the long-awaited Messiah, God's supremely Anointed One?

The key passage here is the question Jesus put to the Jewish leaders gathered before him one day in the Temple. These self-appointed masters of the nation's religious welfare, both Pharisees and Sadducees, had plied him with many questions, vainly attempting to trap him in his answers. Now Jesus had one for them:

> How can they say that the Messiah is David's son? For David himself says in the book of Psalms, "The Lord said to my Lord, Sit at my right hand, till I make your enemies a stool for your feet." David thus calls him Lord; so how is he his son?
>
> *Luke 20:41-44*

Although Jesus was descended from David, and so was his offspring, yet he was also the coming Messiah, and so was his Lord. He was the *root* of David as well as his offspring (Revelation 22:16) and David knew he would reign over the kingdom of God for ever. This is the implication of the title Messiah, and it is very useful, before you cover the redeeming work of Jesus in witness to Muslims, to first establish his pre-eminence over all the other prophets of God. Then the uniqueness of his salvation through his crucifixion, death and resurrection, gains more meaning and significance.

The Suffering Servant Of God

The Messiah came the first time in relative obscurity. Jesus was a lowly man, living in a small village in Galilee, an insignificant district north of Judea, far from the religious heart of the nation. Most of the Jews missed their Messiah because they missed the prophecies of his first coming and focused only on those to be fulfilled at a much later date, which spoke of his eternal glory and rule. It is important, when witnessing to Muslims, to point to the original prophecy where the word *mashiah* is used and from which the title Messiah was derived. It contains a plain statement that he would be struck down in the middle of his course:

> And after sixty-two weeks, an anointed one shall be cut off, and shall have nothing. *Daniel 9:26*

This was a direct warning that God's mashiah would be suddenly struck down and killed - a clear reference to the crucifixion and death of Jesus which caught his disciples by surprise. Here you can quote any of the prophecies we studied of his sufferings from Psalms 22 and 69 and from Isaiah 53 which we have already considered. All of these show that he came the first time to redeem us, to save us from our sins, and to find eternal peace and joy.

On the last night Jesus was with his disciples, shortly before his arrest, trial and crucifixion, he spoke to them at length, knowing his ministry was ending and that the supreme purpose for his coming to earth was about to take place. He faced mocking, vicious scourging, being slapped in his face, a hostile mob, an unjust sentence, a painful crucifixion, six hours of excruciating agony on the cross, and an awful death. Yet he could say to his disciples:

> Peace I leave with you, my peace I give to you; not as the world gives do I give to you. *John 14:27*

> These things I have spoken to you, that my joy may be in you, and that your joy may be full. *John 15:11*

Two expressions here must be noted: *my peace* and *my joy*. At no time before this do we find Jesus using either of these terms. What peace or joy could a man have as he faced such a terrible ordeal and certain death within twenty-four hours? Yet he waited specifically until this moment, when most other men would have been overcome with fear and anguish, to speak of his peace and joy - precisely *because* he was filled with them at a time when the opposite might have been expected.

Although he was about to die, his sole pleasure was to do his Father's will (John 14:31), and he faced the cross with peace and joy because he knew he had come for this purpose and nothing that was to happen to him could disturb his calm assurance that his Father would bring him back to life and that he would rejoice when he saw the fruit of his travail (Isaiah 53:11).

It was his burning love for mankind and his determination to endure whatever it would cost to save us that made him face the cross calmly and resolutely. He knew the Messiah would be cut off at his first coming and would only be crowned with glory at his second coming. In between he offers the hope of his salvation to all men, including all Muslims, which is the *only* way by which anyone can be saved. It is crucial to distinguish these two facets of the Messiah's mission - the first time in humility to save us, the second in glory to transform us. This is what is embodied in the title *al-Masih*, a twofold mission not just to preach the Word of God as other prophets had done before him, but also to die for our sins so that we may be freed from our bondage and be guaranteed a place in the kingdom yet to be revealed.

The Glory of God's Anointed Saviour

It cannot be denied, however, that *glory* is the key characteristic of the Messiah that the Old Testament prophecies foresaw. To some extent this explains why the Israelites overlooked the passages clearly predicting his suffering and obscurity and focused on his glory and triumphant rule instead. Perhaps it was nothing more than the typical human instinct to be seen to be backing a winner. No one wants to be identified with a loser. This is why virtually all Jesus' disciples and followers deserted him when he was arrested and crucified. They had a lot to learn! One of the most difficult tasks of Christian evangelism is to call on the human race to renounce its pride, triumphalism and haughtiness. Unless it does it will never come to the knowledge of truth and this includes all the Muslims of the world. Pride comes before a fall, the proverb says. So also humility comes before honour (Proverbs 15:33).

Nonetheless, having first passed through the valley of Jesus' humiliation and dishonour, we are now equipped to deal with the glory of the Messiah. It has been estimated that there are up to five hundred prophecies of the second coming of Jesus in his eternal glory. The first step was his *resurrection from the dead*. This sets Jesus apart from all the other prophets of God and, let it be said, the Prophet of Islam. Moses was buried by the Lord himself. Muhammad is buried in a tomb which is visited by millions of Muslims every year. The very journey is known as a *ziyarah*, a "visitation." As the Apostle Peter said of the great King David, "he both died, and was buried, and his tomb is with us to this day" (Acts 2:29) and was, no doubt, appropriately venerated.

Jesus, however, has three tombs, a unique qualification in any circumstance. If you visit Jerusalem and the Catholic Church of the Holy

Sepulchre, you will be taken down to a tomb below the ground which is said to be his burial place. Just beyond the Dung Gate at the northern entrance to the old city, however, is a garden with a tomb hewn out of a rock consistent with the tomb of Jesus spoken of in the Gospels (Luke 23:53). The Protestants will tell you that this is the true tomb of Jesus. Make a pilgrimage to Mecca and a *ziyarah* to Medina, however, and you will be shown a tomb of Jesus next to that of Muhammad and his successors Abu Bakr and Umar, where Jesus will supposedly be buried after his return to earth.

Yet he fills none of them! He is alive, in heavenly glory, having *risen* from the dead never to die again. You can make a huge impact on Muslims here. The prophecies of his resurrection which we considered from the Psalms and the prophecies of Isaiah, are a telling testimony to the source of his ultimate glory. He rose from the dead, inconspicuously at first, only to ascend to raven from which he will appear in heavenly glory when he returns to earth.

On the day of his resurrection he appeared to be no more than a normal traveller on the road from Emmaus to Jerusalem. Two of his disciples were walking along the road and, as he drew near to them, he seemed to be no more than an ordinary man out for an ordinary evening's walk. They talked to him about all that had happened over that weekend, especially the fate of Jesus of Nazareth who they had hoped was the Messiah of Israel. When they finished their conversation with confusion at his demise and rumours of his resurrection, he declared:

> O foolish men, and slow of heart to believe all that the prophets have spoken! Was it not necessary that the Messiah should suffer these things and enter into his glory? *Luke 24:25-26*

The resurrection of Jesus from the dead was the prelude of his glory, but there was to be no sign of this while he remained another forty days on earth. It was only at his ascension to heaven that the glory of what he had achieved began to be realised. We will cover this in the last chapter of this book. Here, however, you need to be content with the fact that, right now, the glory of Jesus is, to all intents and purposes, hidden from the eyes of all who do not believe in him, especially Muslims. But you can witness to it! Peter wrote to the early Christians:

> The prophets who prophesied of the grace that was to be yours searched and enquired about this salvation; they inquired what

> person or time was indicated by the Spirit of the Messiah within them when predicting the sufferings of the Messiah and the subsequent glory. *1 Peter 1:10-11*

The subsequent glory! This is where you can witness to Muslims very effectively. The Messiah came the first time in obscurity and died for our salvation. He will come the second time in glory to redeem his own, to raise them from the dead in perfect glory, and take them into his eternal kingdom to be with him for ever and ever. This text foreshadows the great event:

> Behold, he is coming with the clouds, and every eye will see him, every one who pierced him; and all tribes of the earth will wail on account of him. Even so, Amen. Revelation 1:7

Muhammad lies dead and buried in Medina. No one saw him transfigured on a holy mountain. No one witnessed his resurrection from the dead. And no one will witness his triumphant return to earth. As Muslims believe in the return of Jesus, emphasise the wonder and awe it will occasion. He will return in glory. His face will be like the sun shining in full strength (Revelation 1:16). Islamic tradition robs Jesus of his glory, suggesting he appeared as no more than a messenger and that he will return as no more than a servant of Islam. It levels the playing field, claiming that he was no more than an ordinary prophet like all the other prophets of God. Its assessment of Jesus is purely horizontal.

You need to witness to the fact that, with this man, all the issues are *vertical*! From the heights of heaven to the humiliation of a cross. From the depths of the grave to the throne of God in heaven. The finest passage in the New Testament that brings this remarkable distinction into focus begins:

> Though he was in the form of God, he did not count equality with God a thing to be grasped, but emptied himself, taking the form of a servant, being born in the likeness of men. And being found in human form he humbled himself and became obedient unto death, even death on a cross. Philippians 2:6-8

That's the downward spiral which concentrates exclusively on his first coming. Unlike Adam, who sought equality with God, Jesus, who had that equality from all eternity, became a human being and was, during the first thirty years of his life, indistinguishable from other men. Yet, while nothing more was required of Adam than that he should be a humble servant of God, Jesus was required to descend to the dust, to be condemned as a criminal, and be executed in the worst of forms, reserved for the baser nations of the earth and the most heinous of crimes (no Roman citizen was allowed to be humiliated by crucifixion). This vertical descent is important in witness to Muslims. It moves away from the deliberately horizontal nature of Muslim faith and experience. Of course, if it had ended there, it would still have the appearance of nothing more than defeat. But the passage continues:

> Therefore God has highly exalted him and bestowed on him the name which is above every name, that at the name of Jesus every knee should bow, in heaven and on earth and under the earth, and every tongue confess that Jesus Christ is Lord to the glory of God the Father. *Philippians 2:9-11*

This is the ascending scale! From the depths of the grave God raised him, not to a renewed, normal healthy life on earth as if nothing had happened, but to heavenly glory, above all the angels, at the very right hand of the Father, from which he will come to judge the whole human race at the end of time. Jesus Christ will not return to become a follower of Muhammad, he will return to judge Muhammad!

This is the meaning of the title *al-Masih*, the Messiah. He was no ordinary prophet, he was the ultimate figurehead, who came from heaven, who plumbed the depths, only to rise again and scale the heights. He ascended from the earth to heaven, he is alive there to this day (as Islam admits), and he will return in heavenly glory. On that day every man, including all Muslims, will be judged by their relationship *to Jesus*, God's Anointed Messiah. His complete authority over all the earth and the final destiny of all men is finely summed up in this text:

> God raised him from the dead and made him sit at his right hand in the heavenly places, far above all rule and authority and power and dominion, and above every name that is named, not only in this age but also in that which is to come; and he has put all things under his feet and has made him the head over all things for the church, which is his body, the fulness of him who fills all in all.
> *Ephesians 1:2-23*

It may take time, but with receptive Muslims you have much to gain by patiently working through the prophetic history of Israel, concentrating on the great prophecies of a Deliverer to come, who would first suffer and then enter into his glory, and then climaxing with a portrayal of the ultimate glory of God's glorious Messiah who will return to claim his own and judge the rest. Where do the Muslims wish to be on that day? On which side of Jesus will they wish to be (for, at the end of it all, that is all that will matter)? He is God's Supremely Anointed One (as the Qur'an freely admits), he is the Great Deliverer and Saviour, and he will be the Judge on that awesome Day yet to be revealed.

In the simple title *al-Masih*, "the Anointed One," you have a foundation for witness to Muslims, a door to a comprehensive witness of who Jesus really was - and ultimately will be. Use the common ground Islam gives to press on to an effective witness of who our Saviour and Lord really is, and how he is the only one who can redeem the world from its sin, devilishness and ultimate destruction.

The Love of God

Father, Son and Holy Spirit

The First and Great Commandment

How does a Christian ever communicate the Trinity to Muslims? If you use an illustration to explain it, you may be sorely disappointed. One of the favourite representations of the Trinity is water which, though one in substance, can be threefold in its form - steam, water or ice depending on its temperature. If you use this symbolic image for the Trinity, a wise Muslim will retort: "So, when God is steaming hot, he is the Father; when he is at room temperature, he is the Son; and when he is ice cold, he is the Holy Spirit." Don't blame the Muslim, you've invited this sort of ridicule.

The Trinity is not a concept of God, nor can it be illustrated. *It is the revelation of God at the depth of his divine being, and the common denominator is love.* All Muslims will accept the suggestion that human beings are the servants of God, called to obey his commandments and do his will. But there is another dimension here which only believing Christians can know, and it is summed up in this text:

> What does the Lord require of you, but to fear the Lord your God, to walk in all his ways, to love him, to serve the Lord your God with all your heart and with all your soul.
>
> *Deuteronomy 10:12*

The new dimension is summed up in just three words, *to love him*, and as we contemplate these words, we realise that our service to God is not just to be a conformity to duties, such as fixed times of prayer and a once-in-a-lifetime pilgrimage, but a much deeper devotion of the heart towards the God who loves us from the depth of his own being. Even in Old Testament times he spoke of "my eyes and my heart" (1 Kings 9:3) and in the New Testament we see this love fully expressed in Jesus Christ. Here, more than in any other witness source, we have our best opportunity to reveal to Muslims who our God and Father really is.

This is the essential difference between Christianity and Islam. The Muslims strive all their lives, through good works and conformity to Islamic religious prescriptions, to gain the favour of God; yet we begin with that favour impressed upon us and are called to a lifetime of service to others with no regard for our own well-being. For we know his banner over is love (Song of Solomon 2:4) and that nothing can separate us from his love (Romans 8:39).

You have no finer point for witness to Muslims of the glory of the Christian faith, our knowledge of God at the depth of his love for us, than you have here. Muslims are trained to follow the precepts of their religion, believing God will accept them provided they do this in spite of their sins and personal coldness of their hearts towards him. Yet we know that a true devotion consists of a much deeper commitment which is summed up in these words:

> And this is love, that we follow his commandments; this is the commandment, as you have heard from the beginning, that you follow love. *2 John 6*

As the Bible puts it so beautifully, we love, *because he first loved us* (1 John 4:19). We know that our sins are forgiven in Christ, that we have already become children of God, that we have received the Spirit of God, that we know God personally, and that we are the sons and daughters of his kingdom. Why? Because *we know the Triune God.*

In Old Testament times God revealed himself purely as *El-Shaddai*, God Almighty. He also revealed his name, *Yahweh*, the God who is, apart from whom there is no god. But in the New Testament we have a much fuller revelation of God at the depth of his being, a *triune* God who is Father, Son and Holy Spirit, who (as we shall see) is God for us, God with us, and God in us. Never mind theological differences with Muslims, here you have the best opportunity to express to Muslims who God really is and how he desires to enter into a deep personal relationship with them.

The Love of God in the Qur'an

Firstly, let us look at how the Qur'an sees the love of God. The book contains many exhortations to true believers to love God with the assurance that Allah approves of those who are devoted to him. A typical text expressing this equation reads:

> Say, if you love Allah, follow me; Allah will love you and forgive you your sins. *Surah 3:31*

Significantly one does not find, in this text nor in any other in the Qur'an, the command to love God with all one's heart, soul, strength and mind. The reason is that these texts in the Qur'an are only an exhortation to obedience to Allah's commands, and Allah's "love" is really no more than a gesture of approval of the faithful worshipper. The basic object of this love, accordingly, is the acquittal and approval of God for the believer. A few issues here are important in our witness to Muslims:

1. No knowledge of forgiveness and acquittal

The Muslim's devotion is all directed towards one goal - gaining the approval of God when his life is over. He ends where we rejoice to begin! The Qur'an leaves the issue of God's forgiveness undecided. While it teaches that he is *al-Ghaffur*, "the Forgiver," it never assures the Muslim of his total forgiveness for his sins. That remains to be seen in eternity. The Muslim can *strive* for Allah's forgiveness but he can never know it. He therefore strives towards one goal, his ultimate acquittal on the Day of Judgment which he hopes to attain to through his good works and religious devotions. In such circumstances he cannot love God from the depth of his heart. He cannot express such love without some prospect of acquittal and acceptance with God foremost in his soul and mind.

2. No expression of God's love for mankind

The Qur'an says very little substantially about God's love for mankind. Invariably this is defined as no more than an approval of those who do good. This verse is a typical example of the overall teaching of the Qur'an about God's love for mankind:

> Spend your wealth for the cause of Allah, and be not cast by your own hands to ruin; and do good. Lo! Allah loves the beneficent.
> *Surah 2:195*

So Allah's love for mankind is very little different to man's love for him. The Muslim primarily seeks *approval*, and the God of Islam gives that approval to those who are faithful to him. In every case where the expression "love" occurs it can be translated "approves of" rather than "loves" without any change in the meaning of the expression. The knowledge and realisation of this approval will also only be known at the Last Day. This is virtually all that the Qur'an teaches about Allah's love for the human race.

3. The Allah of Islam has no heart

According to Islamic tradition Allah has ninety-nine names. They are all Biblical enough (an equivalent for every one can be found in the Bible), yet they are not part of his essential being. According to Islam they are all no more than *attributes* of Allah and that he can express or withhold them at will. They are not essential to his being. Allah can choose to be faithful, loving, forgiving, accepting and so on. He can just as readily and justifiably choose to be unforgiving, rejecting, displeased and disapproving. It all depends on his own judgment. No man has any claim on him. He can express his attributes at will. No one can accuse him of unfairness for he does what he pleases.

Allah has neither heart nor soul. The great Muslim scholar al-Ghazzali brought this out very clearly in his book *al-Maqsad al-Husna* (The Beautiful Names). He went out of his way to assert that the title *al-Waddud*, "the Loving One," means far less than the title may seem to indicate. Although some of the ninety-nine names of Allah appear regularly in the Qur'an (such as *ar-Rahmaan*, "the Compassionate" and *al-Aziz*, "the Mighty"), this one only appears twice and without significance to the text preceding it (Surahs 11:90, 85:14). Al-Ghazzali explains the love of Allah as consisting solely of *objective* acts of kindness and expressions of approval.

He denied that Allah feels any love for mankind in his heart, stating that he remains above the feeling of love. Quite what that means he does not say, nor does he explain how any being can be a better person by being devoid of heartfelt affection towards other beings, but his interpretation of Allah as the Loving One is quite clear. He added that love and mercy are desired in respect of their objects only for the sake of their fruit and benefit and not because of empathy or feeling.

This explains why the Qur'an omits the Biblical command to love God with all our hearts, souls and minds. Why should we if he doesn't feel the same way towards us in return? Essentially there is nothing in the Allah of Islam that can awaken the response of dedicated affection from mankind in return.

We have to go back to the Bible to discover this very God, the Triune God who allows us to become behind the inner curtain and experience the fulness of his love for us as revealed in the Father who loves us, the Son who died for us, and the Holy Spirit who activates the love of God in our hearts.

God The Father: God for Us

I have already dealt with this subject in Facing the Muslim Challenge (pages 83-86) but it is essential to this book and will cover it again, though from a different perspective. There is no better way of making the God of the Bible attractive to Muslims than the revelation of his love for us in the New Testament knowledge of his Triune being.

We shall begin with the Father. "The Father himself loves you", Jesus told his disciples, (John 16:27), and this love is expressed in the form human beings know best, from a parent to a child. If God is our Father, then we are his children, and the relationship we share with him immediately becomes far deeper than anything any other religion can project. According to Islam a believer can never be greater than a servant of God (Surah 19:93) but children have an authority and closeness to their Father that no servant can hope to attain to. It is summed up in these words of Jesus:

> "What do you think Simon? From whom do kings of the earth take toll or tribute? From their sons or from others?" And when he said "From others," Jesus said to him "then the sons are free."
>
> *Matthew 17:25-26*

Because the Christian believer is a child of God, he is already a lawful member of the household of God (Ephesians 2:19). He does not have to earn his place there, nor can he ever be dismissed from God's kingdom. The children of God are free to enjoy all that their heavenly Father calls his own. They are his heirs along with the supreme heir to the Father's throne, Jesus Christ. A point made to me by a Muslim once, and my reply to it, brings this out very clearly and you should use it in your witness to Muslims.

The Muslim said to me "You Christians reduce the glory of God, you call him your Father and therefore make him out to be little more than yourselves." He continued: "Your Lord's Prayer opens with just two words, Our Father, which shows just how little you honour him." He then quoted the first verses of the Qur'an:

> All praise be to Allah, Lord of the worlds, the Compassionate, the Merciful, Master of the Day of Reckoning.
>
> *Surah 1:2-4*

"See how we glorify Allah," he proclaimed, "see how great is our praise to him! How different to your simple introduction, Our Father." I replied that he had quite rightly discerned one aspect of Christian belief about God, but had completely missed another. "You are quite right when you say our God is not much higher than we are, that the gap between us is very small" I continued, "but you're missing the point. It's not down at our level that the gap is narrow, it's up at his!" I finished by saying that we never made God our Father at any time, rather he made us his children when his own Son died and rose again for our salvation and redemption. We have been raised right up to his level and are declared to be little lower than himself (Psalm 8:4-6).

There is no other religion in the world that relates to God even remotely as close as ours does. We are his heirs! You will know the saying "Like father, like son," and nowhere is this more true than in the person of Jesus Christ who is the exact image of the living God (Colossians 1:15). Yet we too have become the sons and daughters of God and are not just his servants but are constantly being renewed and conformed to his likeness. Another well known expression also applies here: "One day my son this will all be yours." Once again this is perfectly true of the heavenly Father's commitment to his own Son, but because we share in the inheritance of Jesus, his kingdom will one day also be ours as well. It is his good pleasure to give it to us (Luke 12:32). We are not religious people, reciting scriptural texts, performing pilgrimages, going through ritualistic practices, conforming to a pattern of life as Muslims are. We are a *redeemed* people of God, we have been set free from dead works and pointless repetitive ceremonies. We *know* God *personally*, we have entered into his very *presence*, we have an *assured* hope, and we can *bask* in the knowledge of his absolute love for us. We do not hope for forgiveness, we *have* it.

Bilquis Sheikh titled her testimony of conversion to Christ *I Dared to Call Him Father*. It is because of this intensely close relationship that we know that God is for us, he has predetermined our destiny. Knowing God as Father is one of the finest ways you can convey the love of God and our experience of his glory to Muslims. Ours is not a concept of God, it is a living knowledge of his eternal being. We do not simply believe in God, *he believes in us!*

God the Son: God with Us

Jesus Christ was not just the final messenger of God, he is also God's final message to mankind! John's Gospel more than any of the other three focuses on the unique revelation of the Triune God in the knowledge of Jesus Christ. John concentrates on teachings of Jesus about God as Father, himself as his Son, and the Holy Spirit. He knew that Jesus had come to open the door, to make God known, and to express his very presence with us on earth.

The Word was in the beginning. The Word was with God, and the Word was God. And the Word became flesh and dwelt among us (John 1:1,14). "God has visited his people!" the Jews declared as Jesus walked among them (Luke 7:16). Indeed he had. Jesus among us was God with us. The most famous verse in the New Testament defines just what this means. One little word, which I shall emphasise, brings this out very emphatically:

> For God *so* loved the world that he gave his only Son, that whoever believes in him should not perish but have eternal life.
>
> *John 3:16*

Here you have once again the heart of the Christian Gospel, the essential basis of all our witness to Muslims. The Qur'an has very little to say about the love of God other than to use the word as an expression of approval, and it is little wonder when it denies the fact that Jesus is the Son of God and that he died for our sins. It has denied the greatest manifestation of God's love that could ever have been given to mankind. As Jesus said:

> Greater love has no man than this, that a man lay down his life for his friends. *John 15:13*

This is the greatest and most abiding form of love, love that is as strong as death (Song of Solomon 8:6) and cannot be overcome by it. Such love was revealed at its fullest extent when Jesus willingly laid down his life:

> When Jesus knew that his hour had come to depart out of the world to the Father, having loved his own who were in the world, he loved them to the end. *John 13:1*

So we see the love of the Father for us in being willing to make us children and the love of the Son by laying down his life so that we might receive the full forgiveness of our sins and so become the sons and daughters of God. Let us see, in closing, how God applies this love to us by the Holy Spirit who enters into our very own beings.

God the Spirit: God in Us

This is where we actually experience the love of God towards us. This is where it becomes real to us. In a nutshell the following passage defines this principle:

> But when the time had fully come, God sent forth his Son, born of a woman, born under the law, to redeem those who were under the law, so that we might receive adoption as sons. And because you are sons God has sent the Spirit of his Son into our hearts, crying, "Abba! Father!." *Galatians 4:4-6*

This is, perhaps, the most remarkable evidence of God's love towards us. Christians actually *know* God, his Spirit lives *within* them. This activates a personal awareness of the love of God in Christ towards us and makes us experience a living relationship with God. Ultimately the difference between those who are approved by God and those who are not is not just a matter of conviction and belief. It is a difference of mega proportions. God actually dwells in believers as opposed to unbelievers who are contaminated by their sins. It is not a certificate of assurance that we have informing us that our sins are forgiven. We are *united* to God. His Spirit dwells in the depths of our being. We are joined to God in a relationship that can never be broken.

Much the same is taught in the following verse where the presence of the indwelling Spirit makes us conscious of our relationship with God:

> When we cry "Abba! Father!," it is the Spirit himself bearing witness with our spirit that we are children of God, and if children, then heirs, heirs of God and fellow heirs with Christ, provided we suffer with him in order that we may also be glorified with him.
> *Romans 8:15-17*

The issues between Muslims and Christians do not focus on the identity of God. Our message to the Muslims is not that they worship a false god and that must now come and worship the true God. Not at all. It's a question of the depth of the revelation of God's love towards us. In Christ we have gained an access to God which brings us into the very depth of his divine presence and here we discover the Triune nature of God and its essential basis - his everlasting love for us.

When we witness to Muslims we are calling them away from the mechanics of lip service to God. We are encouraging them to abandon the repetitive rituals they slavishly follow day after day, such as the monotonous *salaat* which is little more than an exercise of physical devotions, mundanely performed with the same endless routines. We are encouraging them to come into a living relationship with God where they can experience his forgiveness and divine presence in their hearts, challenging them daily to forsake all sinfulness, opportunism, selfishness and deceit; so that they may become like God in his perfect purity and righteousness and be prepared for a kingdom of perfect holiness.

Our message to the Muslims is this: we have come to know God, we have been *forgiven* by God, we have been adopted as the eternal children of God, we have received the *Spirit* of God, we are heirs of the *kingdom* of God. This is what the Gospel really is, not a presentation of correct beliefs or a formula to draw ear to God, but a deep call to a living knowledge of God and the assurance of a place in his eternal kingdom when it will be revealed at the end of time. The Holy Spirit within us is the "guarantee of our inheritance until we acquire possession of it, to the praise of his glory" (Ephesians 1:14).

This is why Christians can afford to be humble rather than arrogant. This is why we can be satisfied with our worship without having to prove anything to ourselves. The seal of God is upon us. We have nothing to prove. We *are* God's children now. We have the deep *assurance* of his love towards us. This is not something we one day hope will work our way. The indwelling Spirit has given us the definite knowledge that we are God's children now and that our place in his eternal kingdom is an absolute certainty. We do not hope for God's approval on the Day of Judgment, we know that that day will be the moment of our glorification as we are joined with Jesus Christ to reign over his kingdom for all eternity. This certainty is beautifully emphasised in these two texts:

> Hope does not disappoint us, because God's love has been poured into our hearts through the Holy Spirit which has been given to us.
> *Romans 5:5*

> So then you are no longer strangers and sojourners, but you are fellow citizens with the saints and members of the household of

> God, built upon the foundation of the apostles and prophets, Christ Jesus himself being the cornerstone, in whom the whole structure is joined together and grows into a holy temple in the Lord, in whom you also are built into it for a dwelling place of God in the Spirit. *Ephesians 2:19-22*

Muslims often think the Trinity is a self-evident fallacy, the great weakness of the Christian faith. On the contrary it is our greatest strength. It reveals the depth of God's love towards us and our opportunity to know him personally. The *Father* opens the door for us to draw closer to God than the adherents of any other religion could ever have imagined, the *Son* through his redeeming death and resurrection has made it possible for us to be forgiven of all our sins right now, and the *Spirit* has entered our hearts to join us even now to God in an absolute oneness of being.

The Muslim *hopes* to be forgiven on the Day of Judgment and directs all his devotion and service towards this end; the Christian *knows* he is forgiven and lives out his life in heartfelt service to God, seeking no favours for himself but the welfare of others. We begin where Muslims hope to end!

Nuzul-I-Isa

The Second Coming of Jesus

Implications of the Return of Jesus to Earth

One of the great beliefs Christians and Muslims hold in common is the eventual return of Jesus Christ to earth. Although we may differ in our understanding of the events that led up to his ascension to heaven, we both agree that he was taken up alive at the end of his earthly life and will return from heaven at the end of this age. Here again there are differences in our convictions about how he will appear and what he will come to accomplish, but the very fact of his return is a crucial meeting-point between Christians and Muslims and one we can build on in our witness to them.

On the last night that he was with his disciples, during the famous Last Supper just before his crucifixion, Jesus had a very intimate conversation with his disciples. He revealed to them deeper truths than he had done at any other time during his ministry. The whole text of this dialogue is found in the thirteenth to the sixteenth chapters of John's Gospel and many of his statements touched on his ultimate return to earth. He began:

> In my Father's house are many rooms; if it were not so, would I have told you that I go to prepare a place for you? And when I go and prepare a place for you, I will come again and take you to myself, that where I am you may be also. *John 14:2-3*

"I will come again" was his promise, one he repeated again and again that evening. "I will not leave you desolate, I will come to you," he added (John 14:18). "So you have sorrow now, but I will see you again and your hearts will rejoice; and no one will take your joy from you" - another statement that he would return (John 16:22). Later the same evening, when he stood before the Jewish High Priest Caiaphas, he testified:

> But I tell you, hereafter you will see the Son of man seated at the right hand of Power, and coming on the clouds of heaven.
> *Matthew 26:64*

He kept emphasising this theme as a comfort to his followers and a warning to his foes. He taught plainly that his return would herald the Day of Judgment and that all mankind would be separated into two camps, some for glory, others for damnation. Their attitude to him would determine their destiny. His followers would join him in the kingdom of heaven, the rest would be cast into eternal darkness. He summed this up in these words:

> When the Son of man comes in his glory, and all the angels with him, then he will sit on his glorious throne. Before him will be gathered all the nations, and he will separate them one from another as a shepherd separates the sheep from the goats, and he will place the sheep at his right hand, and the goats at the left.
> *Matthew 25:31-32*

The Qur'an does not teach the second coming of Jesus in such emphatic language but as we have seen the Muslim world has long held that the following verse, which we considered in an earlier chapter, specifically refers to the return of Jesus to the earth:

> And there is knowledge of the hour. *Surah 43:61*

This is the literal translation of the text, though Muslim scholars state that, as the immediately preceding texts cover the subject of Jesus, this text is a conclusion to the narrative, and Yusuf Ali, filling in the gaps in brackets, translates it: "And (Jesus) shall be a Sign (for the coming of) the Hour (of Judgment). A record from the Hadith gives the Muslim position on the purpose of his return:

> Abu Huraira reported that the Messenger of Allah (pbuh) said: By Him in Whose hand is my life, the son of Mary (pbuh) will soon descend among you as a just judge. He will break crosses, kill swine and abolish Jizya, and wealth will pour forth to such an extent that no one will accept it. *Sahih Muslim, Vol.1. p.92*

Muslims believe Jesus will return to destroy the Antichrist and his hosts, that he will turn all men and women on earth into followers of Islam, and that he will usher in an age of unprecedented prosperity. We do not agree with this expectation, but the important point in witness to Muslims is the mere *fact* of his return, and here Christians have tremendous material for witness of his glory and eternal purposes.

The idea that a human being ascended alive to heaven two thousand years ago, has lived there in perfect health ever since, and will one day come back to earth, begs further scrutiny. The event will be totally unique and its climactic character begs the conclusion that there must be something very special about the man Jesus Christ. During their lifetimes all the prophets only influenced their immediate environment and age, yet Jesus will return to transform the earth and radically affect all the nations scattered across it. What is it about him that will result in such an awesome event at the end of time?

Perhaps the answer lies in the expression used by many Muslim commentators on the Qur'an, such as Yusuf Ali and Maulana Daryabadi. They speak of the *second* coming of Jesus, a common Christian expression to describe his return. We use the expression "second coming" *because we believe he came from heaven the first time as well.* If there is to be a second coming, there must have been a first coming. If Muslims tell you they believe in the second coming, challenge them about the implications of this description. Jesus himself is the source of our conviction that he came from heaven the first time as well. He is recorded as saying:

> For I have come down from heaven, not to do my own will, but the will of him who sent me. *John 6:38*

In response to this the Jews asked: "How does he now say, I have come down from heaven?" (John 6.42). When even some of his own followers began to murmur at his teaching he said to them:

> Do you take offence at this? Then what if you were to see the Son of man ascending where he was before? *John 6:61-62*

He regularly stated that he was no ordinary human being but had come down from heaven. "I am from above ... I am not of this world" (John 8:23). This is why he returned to heaven at the end of his earthly life - because he had come from there in the first place! He summed it all up in one emphatic statement:

> I came from the Father and have come into the world; again, I am leaving the world and going to the Father. *John 16:28*

All other men, both small and great, including Enoch and Elijah, have returned whence they came. "No one has ascended into heaven, but he who descended from heaven," Jesus proclaimed (John 3:13). Moses was buried by the Lord, David lies buried in Jerusalem, and even Muhammad, the Prophet of Islam, whom Muslims believe to be the last and greatest of God's messengers, lies buried in Medina. None of them lived beyond a normal lifespan, nor did Abraham, Joseph or any others of the great prophets of old. Why, then, did this one man ascend to heaven to remain alive there, the only living man among myriads of angels, until he returns to earth at the end of time?

There can only be one logical conclusion. He returned to heaven *because he came from there in the first place*. Muslims speak of the *nuzul-i-Isa*, the "descension of Jesus," to describe his second coming. What the Bible shows is that it will be very similar to his first *nuzul*, his first descension to earth when he became the man Jesus of Nazareth. We do not have to rely on speculations here because, as we have seen, he himself taught that he was in heaven before the world began. A passage of scripture says "He is before all things, and in him all things hold together" (Colossians 1:17). Jesus confirmed this when he said:

> I saw Satan fall like lightning from heaven. *Luke 10:18*

According to the Bible the fall of Satan took place when he attempted to usurp the throne of God in heaven and make himself like the Most High (Isaiah 14:14). This took place before the creation of Adam and Eve, which is obvious because, when he tempted them, he had already become the greatest of all devils. The Qur'an places the fall of the great *Shaytaan*, whom it names *Iblis* (which is derived from the original Greek word which gives us our word "diabolical"), at the beginning of creation, saying that he refused to bow to Adam at God's command (Surah 2:34), complaining that Adam had only been made of dust while he had been made of fire (Surah 7:18). Nonetheless both books place Satan's fall at a very early age and Jesus emphatically stated "I was there, I saw it happen."

On another occasion Jesus declared that he had shared his Father's glory "before the world was made" (John 17:5), another statement confirming that he had been in heaven for ages before he came to earth. From these statements we can explain to Muslims why he is going to return to earth and, once the uniqueness of his two comings is fully appreciated, you can move on to reveal to them precisely who Jesus really is and why he will one day come back to call the whole earth, both the dead and the living, to the day of destiny and the separation of all men to eternal life or everlasting condemnation. An important point here is how Jesus will appear when he returns, and we will proceed to examine this question first before moving on to the full implications of his second coming.

How Jesus will be Identified on His Return

Muslims believe Jesus will return to the great mosque of Damascus in Syria and that he will land on one of its minarets before coming down to earth. I have often asked Muslims how Jesus could be identified on his return if he was to return as no more than an ordinary man. If someone was to appear in Syria and be interviewed one day on TV, claiming "I am Isa. I returned from heaven earlier today. No one saw me but here I am," how would anyone know it really was him? Some Muslims, aware of the need to be able to positively identify him, believe he will have a bone missing in one of his fingers. This is no more than a typical myth but it does show the problem of identifying any ordinary, bearded man dressed in white, as Jesus if he claims to be him. Significantly there is a tradition in Islam telling Muslims how to recognise him. Muhammad is recorded as saying:

> There is no prophet between me and him, that is, Jesus (pbuh). He will descend (to the earth). When you see him, recognise him: a man of medium height, reddish hair, wearing two light yellow garments, looking as if drops were falling down from his head though it will not be wet. *Sunan Abu Dawud, Vol.3, p.1203*

A Muslim friend of mine once said to me "When Jesus comes I believe he will come from heaven shining like a light." I replied, "Why do you say this? This is what Christians believe." He answered "Look where he is coming from. You cannot come from heaven looking like this," pointing to himself. He made a crucial point. The issue is not whether Jesus will return to Damascus, Mecca or Jerusalem, the question is where he is coming from. He will be *coming from heaven*. Having been alive there for thousands of years it is highly unlikely that he will come back in an ordinary, earthly form. Coming from heaven, *he will surely bear the glory of heaven*. Jesus himself confirmed that he will return in heavenly splendour in these words:

> Immediately after the tribulation of those days the sun will be darkened, and the moon will not give its light, and the stars will fall from heaven, and the powers of the heaven will be shaken; then

> will appear the sign of the Son of man in heaven, and then all the tribes of the earth will mourn, and they will see the Son of man coming on the clouds of heaven with power and great glory; and he will send out his angels with a loud trumpet call, and they will gather his elect from the four winds, from one end of heaven to the other. *Matthew 24:29-31*

When even the sun casts a shadow a new brightness will appear. All the earth will see the glory and power of Jesus as the heavens are opened and his presence fills the skies. His light will be so splendid that even the stars and galaxies will recede before him. This is one of the greatest facts about the second coming of Jesus that you need to emphasise with Muslims and you have the testimony of Jesus himself to support it.

This will not be something entirely new. When the Apostle Paul saw Jesus in a heavenly vision on the road to Damascus, a light from heaven, *brighter than the sun*, shone around him and those who were with him (Acts 26:13). When the Apostle John had a vision of the glorified Christ on the island of Patmos, "his face was like the sun shining in full strength" (Revelation 1:16). Even while he was on earth he gave three of his disciples, Peter, James and John, a vision of his heavenly glory as he was transfigured before them. "His face shone like the sun, and his garments became white as light." (Matthew 17:2).

We have no doubt therefore how he will be recognised when he returns. *No one will fail to recognise him.* He will not descend as a man of flesh and blood, he will be revealed from heaven in all his splendour. Another key text can be quoted here:

> Behold, he is coming with the clouds, and every eye will see him, every one who pierced him; and all tribes of the earth will wail on account of him. Even so, Amen. *Revelation 1:7*

More than five billion people currently populate the earth. Billions of others have been buried in previous generations. Prophets and saints, kings and tyrants, small and great, have all alike perished and gone back to the dust from whence they came. But right now one man is alive in heaven where he ascended and from where he will return. He has been there almost two thousand years whereas very few other men ever reach a hundred years. It is surely absurd to believe that he is, to this day, nothing more than an ordinary human being.

As I have already mentioned, I have often chatted with Muslims about the fact that Jesus is the only person who ever lived who has three tombs on earth (Two in Jerusalem and one in Medina). Three tombs for one man! *Yet Jesus fills none of them* and never will. They can dig a thousand graves for Jesus and will be wasting useful energy.

> For we know that Christ being raised from the dead will never die again; death no longer has dominion over him.
>
> *Romans 6:9*

If Jesus had not died but had simply been raptured alive to heaven as Muslims believe, there would have been no point keeping him there once those who sought his life had passed away. He should have been sent back to earth to complete his mission. This is exactly what happened when Herod sought to kill him when he was only two years old. When Herod died, however, Jesus and his family returned from Egypt to Galilee in Israel (Matthew 2:21). The ascension of Jesus to heaven *after* his death and resurrection, however, makes much more sense and it explains why he has been alive in heaven, in perfect health, ever since. He is *glorified* in heaven, and it is from the same heaven, with the same glory, that he will return. Impress this glorious truth on Muslims.

The First and Second Comings of Jesus

I believe, however, that the most effective Christian witness at this point to Muslims centres on the two advents of Jesus on earth taken together. One needs to look at the second coming in context with his first coming. We have already seen that Jesus plainly taught that he came from heaven in the first place. He consistently also taught that he would return to heaven, a fact which is not only confirmed in the Bible but is believed universally by Muslims. He will return from heaven to earth at the end of time.

The key question here for Muslims is why Jesus dwelt on the earth for such a short period of only thirty-three years when he had spent millennia in heaven before this and has done so ever since. There must have been a *special* purpose for his coming to earth the first time. You can give the Muslims two fundamental reasons for his appearance on earth as an ordinary human being two millennia ago.

Firstly, *he came to bridge the gap between heaven and earth*, between the God of holiness and sinful men. No one has beaten death and ascended to heaven to live there for ever (John 3:13). All men die and wither as their bodies decay in the ground. A chasm exists between heaven and earth for this reason:

> Behold, the Lord's hand is not shortened, that it cannot save, or his ear dull, that it cannot hear; but your iniquities have made a separation between you and your God, and your sins have hid his face from you, so that he does not hear. *Isaiah 59:1-2*

The God of heaven dwells in unapproachable light with his holy angels. Sinful men and women on earth cannot enter the portals of the Most High. Muslims believe that, when Adam and Eve were driven from the Garden of Eden for their transgression, they were subsequently forgiven, but they were never let back into the Garden. They died and perished like all their descendants do. Jesus came *from* heaven to close the gap which we could not bridge from earth. He did this *by bringing something of heaven into this world*, namely himself. The divine spirit of the second person of the Triune God took human form and, by uniting man to God and God to man, brought the presence of God in human form to all humans who walk the face of this lonely planet.

Secondly, *he bridged the gap between earth and heaven by dying for our sins as an ordinary human being*. On the cross he endured the wrath of God against universal human sin so that we could be forgiven, be born of the Spirit of God, and eventually be transformed ourselves into heavenly beings who will ascend likewise to the eternal heavenly realm where we too will live for ever! To do this Jesus had to become like us. Because we are only flesh and blood, "he himself likewise partook of the same nature" (Hebrews 2:14). He came "in the likeness of sinful flesh" (Romans 8:3) to redeem it. He has become the mediator between man and God and, by his death and resurrection, has become the door through which we can walk into the highest heavens where our God and Father dwells.

> Therefore he had to be made like his brethren in every respect, so that he might become a merciful and faithful high priest in the service of God, to make expiation for the sins of the people.
> *Hebrews 2:17*

Jesus did not come like some alien Superman who can fly through the skies at his own discretion, exercise awesome physical power to achieve his purposes, and be immune to all diseases, bullets and bombs. He became like us in every respect. He assumed the very weaknesses of our human nature, and ultimately he died as we will die. He bridged the gap between God and men from *both* sides - from heaven to earth by becoming a human being, and from earth to heaven by conquering sin and death on the cross.

Muslims believe Jesus did not complete his earthly mission and must return to do so. In denying his crucifixion, death and resurrection, it is no wonder it misses the accomplishment of his task. Reveal to Muslims how this was the supreme work for which Jesus came and it was the greatest victory any human being has ever achieved on earth - *to conquer death.* As he approached his crucifixion he asked:

> And what shall I say? Father, save me from this hour? No, for this purpose I have come to this hour. *John 12:27*

As he died he cried out: *Accomplished*! (John 19:30). Most translations mitigate the force of the single Greek word (usually in this form: "It is finished!"). No, in a remarkable way, one his disciples could not possibly have discerned at the time, his sudden, unexpected, humiliating death *was itself* the victory to surpass all others and would be confirmed three days later when he rose from the dead.

Jesus came to earth the first time to become just like us in every respect to save us from our sins. Yet, when he returns the second time in all his heavenly glory, *he will come to make us like himself.* We have seen how many texts speak of Jesus shining like the sun in full strength in his heavenly splendour. This is precisely what he says will happen to us when he returns to earth:

> Then the righteous will shine like the sun in the kingdom of their Father. *Matthew 13:43*

He came the first time in all humility in ordinary human form to redeem us from our sins. He will return the second time in all his glory so that we might share it with him. He brought himself down the first time to earth. He will take us to himself in the heavenly realms when he returns the second time. In your witness to Muslims emphasise the fact of the *second coming* and how it inevitably links to his first coming. Show Muslims how they too can become partakers of the divine nature and receive the forgiveness of their sins by becoming disciples of Jesus now, and how they can be transformed when he returns and be raised with the same glory he presently radiates.

The *nuzul-i-Isa* in Islam, his second coming to earth, is a tremendous point of common ground for a very effective witness to Muslims.

Bibliography

1. Christian Books on Muslim Evangelism

Abdul-Haqq, Abdiyah Akbar. *Sharing your Faith with a Muslim.* Bethany Fellowship Inc., Minneapolis, Minnesota, United States of America. 1980

Abd al-Masih. *The Main Challenges for Committed Christians in Serving Muslims.* Light of Life, Villach, Austria. 1996

Addison, James Thayer. *The Christian Approach to the Moslem.* AMS Press Inc., New York, United States of America. 1966

Anonymous. *Christian Witness Among Muslims.* Africa Christian Press, Accra, Ghana, 1971

Bevan Jones, L. *Christianity Explained to Muslims.* YMCA Publishing House, Calcutta, India. 1952

Challen, Ed. *To Love a Muslim!* Grace Publications, London, England. 1988

Christensen, Jens. *The Practical Approach to Muslims.* North Africa Mission, Marseille, France. 1977

Crossley, John. *Explaining the Gospel to Muslims.* United Society for Christian Literature, London, United Kingdom. 1971

Dennett, Bill. *Sharing the Good News with Muslims.* Anzea Publishers, Homebush West, Australia. 1992.

Dretke, Jim. *A Christian Approach to Muslims.* William Carey Library, Pasadena, California, United States of America. 1979

Elder, J. *The Biblical Approach to the Muslim.* Leadership Instruction and Training International, Houston, Texas, United States of America.

Foreign Missions Conference of N. America. *Christian Literature in Moslem Lands.* George H. Doran Company, New York, United States of America. 1923

Gilchrist, John. *The Christian Witness to the Muslim.* Jesus to the Muslims, Benoni, South Africa. 1988

Goldsmith, Martin. *Islam and Christian Witness.* Hodder and Stoughton, STL Books, Bromley, Kent, United Kingdom. 1982

Haddad, Yvonne Yazbeck and Wadi Z. *Christian-Muslim Encounters.* University Press of Florida, Gainesville, Florida, United States of America. 1995

Haines, John. *Good News for Muslims.* Middle East Resources, Philadelphia, Pennsylvania, United States of America. 1998

Harris, George K. *How to Lead Moslems to Christ.* China Inland Mission, Philadelphia, United States of America. 1957

Madany, Bassam M. *The Bible and Islam: Sharing God's Word with a Muslim.* The Back to God Hour, Palos Heights, Illinois, United States of America. 1981

Mallouhi, Christine A. *Waging Peace on Islam.* Monarch Books, London, United Kingdom. 2000

Marsh, C.R. *Share your Faith with a Muslim.* Moody Press, Chicago, United States of America. 1975

Miller, William M. *A Christian's Response to Islam.* Presbyterian and Reformed Publishing Co., Nutley, New Jersey, United States of America. 1976

Muller, Roland. *Tools for Muslim Evangelism.* Essence Publishing, Belleville, Ontario, Canada. 2000

Nickel, Gordon D. *Peaceable Witness Among Muslims.* Herald Press, Waterloo, Ontario, Canada. 1999

Nehls, Gerhard. *And What About the Muslim?* Evangelical Mission Press, Bellville, South Africa.

Nehls, Gerhard. *Premises and Principles of Muslim Evangelism.* Life Challenge, Bombay, India. 1991.

Nehls, Gerhard. *The Great Commission, You and the Muslims.* Life Challenge, Cape Town, South Africa.

Oksnevad, Roy and Welliver, Dotsey. *The Gospel for Islam.* Evangelism and Missions Information Service, Wheaton, Illinois, United States of America. 2001.

Parshall, Phil. *The Last Great Frontier: Essays on Muslim Evangelism.* Open Doors with Brother Andrew, Quezon City, Philippines. 2000.

Powell, Avril Ann. *Muslims & Missionaries in Pre-Mutiny India.* Curzon Press Ltd., Richmond, Surrey, United Kinmgdom. 1993

Register, Ray G. *Dialogue and Interfaith Witness with Muslims.* Moody Books Inc., Kingsport, Tennessee, United States of America. 1979

Saal, William J. *Reaching Muslims for Christ.* Moody Press, Chicago, United States of America. 1993

Tanagho, Samy. *Glad News! God Loves You, My Muslim Friend.* Calvary Chapel, Santa Ana, California, United States of America. 1999

Vander Werff, Lyle. *Christian Mission to Muslims.* William Carey Library, Pasadena, California, United States of America. 1977

2. Testimonies and Biographies of Muslim Converts

Alam, Christopher. *Through the Blood and the Fire: From Muslim to Born Again Christian.* New Wine Press, Chichester, West Sussex, United Kingdom. 1994

Esther, Gulshan. *The Torn Veil.* Marshall, Morgan & Scott, Basingstoke, United Kingdom. 1984

Esther, Gulshan. *Beyond the Veil.* Marshall Pickering, Hammersmith, London, United Kingdom. 1992

Farnham, Dr. Bruce. *My Big Father.* STL Books, Bromley, Kent, United Kingdom. 1986

Gaudeul, Jean-Marie. *Called from Islam to Christ.* Monarch Books, Crowborough, East Sussex, United Kingdom. 1999

Hanna, Mark. *The True Path: Seven Muslims Make Their Greatest Discovery.* International Doorways Publications, Colorado Springs, Colorado, United States of America. 1975

Hirji-Walji, Hass (and Jaryl Strong). *Escape from Islam.* Kingsway Publications, Eastbourne, United Kingdom. 1981

Lotfi, Nasser. *Iranian Christian.* Word Books, Waco, Texas, United States of America. 1980.

Masood, Steven. *Into the Light.* STL Books, Bromley, Kent, United Kingdom. 1986

Miller, William McElwee. *Ten Muslims Meet Christ.* William B. Eerdman's Publishing Company, Grand Rapids, Michigan, United States of America. 1976

Rasooli, Jay M., and Allen, Cady H. *Dr. Sa'eed of Iran.* William Carey Library, Pasadena, California, United States of America. 1983

Sabri, Reza (with Timothy Sheaff). *Reza: A Moslem Sees Christ.* IMF PUblication, Denton, Texas, United States of America. 1991

Safa, Reza F. *Blood of the Sword, Blood of the Cross: A Fanatical Muslim Tells His Story.* STL Books, Bromley, Kent, United Kingdom.

Sheikh, Bilquis. *I Dared to Call Him Father.* Chosen Books, Waco, Texas, United States of America. 1978

Wootton, R.W.F. *Jesus: More than a Prophet.* STL Books, Bromley, Kent, United Kingdom. 1982

3. Christian Booklets on Muslim Evangelism

Abd al-Masih. *Why is it Difficult for a Muslim to Become a Christian?* Ev. Karmelmission, Schorndorf, Germany.

Akbar Haqq, Dr. A. *Sharing the Lord Jesus Christ with Muslim Neighbours*. Publisher not named. 1978

Anonymous. *Reaching Muslims Today*. North Africa Mission, Upper Darby, Pennsylvania, United States of America. 1976

Hahn, Ernest. *How to Respond to Muslims*. Concordia Publishing House, St. Louis, United States of America. 1995

Hosmon, Sarah L. *Presenting Jesus Christ the Son of God to Moslems*. The India Bible Christian Council, Kanpur, Uttar Pradesh, India. 1956

Jadeed, Iskander. *How to Share the Gospel with our Muslim Brothers*. Light of Life, Villach, Austria.

Kingsriter, Del. *Sharing your Faith with Muslims*. Centre for Ministry to Muslims, Minneapolis, United States of America.

Marrison, G.E. *The Christian Approach to the Muslim*. Lutterworth Press, London, United Kingdom. 1971

Stacey, Vivienne. *Practical Lessons for Evangelism among Muslims*. Orientdienst eV., Wiesbaden, Germany.

4.Booklets of Testimonies of Muslim Coinverts

Alavi, K.K. *In Search of Assurance*. The Good Way, Rikon, Switzerland.

Ambrie, Hamran. *God has Chosen for me Everlasting Life*. The Good Way, Rikon, Switzerland.

El-Ilodigwe, Nasir Suleiman. *From Muslim Scholar to Evangelist*. Fireliners International, Ibadan, Nigeria. 1991

Hakkeem, A. Abdul. *On the Way of the Cross*. Nur ul Alam, Kerala, Manjeri, India.1986

Jan, Tamur. *Ex Muslims for Christ*. The Crossbearers, Birmingham, United Kingdom. 1980

Naaman, Ghulam Masih. *My Grace is Sufficient for You*. The Good Way, Rikon, Switzerland.

Paul, Sultan Muhammed. *Why I Became a Christian*. The Good Way, Rikon, Switzerland.

Subhan, J.A. *How a Sufi Found his Lord*. Lucknow Publishing House, Lucknow, India. 1952

What Others Have to Say About *The Commands of Messiah*:

"Knowing both Richard Burr and Dr. Fleagle well, I know they both have a keen interest in and passion for studying and teaching on the commands of our Lord as steps toward holiness, or becoming more like Him. Thus, they write on the subject with insight, thoroughness, and clarity. All who would follow Jesus and seek to please Him can profit from their teaching and guidance toward knowing and obeying our Lord's commands, and so toward personal holiness, which should be the passion of us all."

Steve Westbrook
President, Pray-Think-Act Ministries, Inc.

"*The Commands of Messiah* is a well-written book that provides many important points from Jesus' teaching which are backed up by many examples. The authors employed parables throughout the book as an enjoyable and effective way of clarifying and illustrating truth."

Harry Mundorff
Retired Teacher and Baseball Coach

"In a day when the Savior's words are often seen as suggestions, *The Commands of Messiah* reminds us with clarity of the Christian's charge, and stands as a dynamic and digestible compendium for the disciple. This is a book to be often recommended and just as often reread!"

Nathan McKeen
Senior Pastor, Flushing Ohio Alliance Church